INSIGHT COMPACT GUIDES

NewYork

Compact Guide: New York City is the perfect quick-reference guide to one of the world's most stimulating cities. It tells you all you need to know about New York's great attractions, from the World Trade Center to Chinatown, from Greenwich Village to the Guggenheim Museum.

This is just one title in *Apa Publications'* new series of pocket-sized, easy-to-use guidebooks intended for the independent-minded traveller. Based on an award-winning formula pioneered in Germany, *Compact Guides* pride themselves on being up-to-date and authoritative. They are in essence mini travel encyclopedias, designed to be comprehensive yet portable, both readable and reliable.

GRAND CENTRAL
TERMINAL

Star Attractions

An instant reference to some of New York's most popular tourist attractions to help you on your way.

World Trade Center p16

Ellis Island p21

Brooklyn Bridge p27

Chinatown p31

Greenwich Village p38

Empire State Building p45

Museum of Modern Art p52

Metropolitan Museum of Art p65

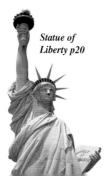

Statue of Liberty p20

Guggenheim Museum p66

American Museum of Natural History p70

NewYork

New York – The City That Never Sleeps

Lower Broadway bustle

If you are traveling to New York for the first time: expect anything to happen, except boredom. The only emotion the place does not arouse is indifference.

'What is barely hinted at in other American cities is condensed and enlarged in New York,' said the writer Saul Bellow. True enough. Since its purchase by the Dutch in 1626, through its growth as a maritime hub, fueled by cheap immigrant labor, to its contemporary position as, arguably, the cultural and retail center of the world, New York has become a city that can't be ignored.

Culturally, it has over 150 museums, including the third largest in the world (the Metropolitan Museum of Art), around 400 art galleries, and over 240 theaters. Broadway and the Metropolitan Opera are famous the world over.

The entertainment possibilities in 'the city that never sleeps' are immense: there's a choice of over 60 clubs, offering everything from jazz to blues, and over 50 places to dance each night of the week. Hungry? There are more than 17,000 different places to eat. Amid all the bustle, there are quiet places too: the city has over 26,000 acres (10,500ha) of parks, the most important and famous of which is Central Park.

5

A night on the town

On the less positive side there's the hectic pace of life, the seasonal extremes of temperature, the crime, the dirt and the poor public services. The streets are in disastrous condition, the sewage system is in disrepair, and the subway trains have a habit of getting stuck in tunnels. Added to this there's the social misery: the homeless are just as much a part of the city as its soaring skyscrapers and oversized limousines.

But New York can't be explained just in terms of its extremes. It's New Yorkers themselves who make this city so exciting. There is a reason why well-known publicity-shy figures, like Greta Garbo and Jacqueline Onassis, chose New York as their home. It's the same reason that Patrick and Brigid of Dublin, or Carlo and Luciana of Venice, might pack their bags and head here some day. New York is the place where ordinary people can, if they are willing to be lucky, become stars, by performing in Washington Square Park, or by making it big in industry, and the place where real stars can walk down the street unnoticed. Or so we are lead to believe: New York is the city of myths, and making them is a part of it. True, New Yorkers do have a reputation for being hurried, even rude, but under their frequent brusqueness is a great sense of humor. Just remember, normality bores them – spontaneity delights them.

New York is a fast-paced town whose residents are possessed of a restless energy. Few people seem to have time

for anything not on their mental schedule; even asking for directions in the street is best done with an awareness of this, ideally while moving at the same pace and in the same direction as the informant.

New Yorkers have persuaded themselves that living at breakneck speed, under constant pressure, is stimulating. This is what gives them their edge and makes Manhattan the center of the universe (which all New Yorkers believe implicitly). It also helps to explain why few people, if they can help it, choose to live out their declining years in the city.

Location and Size

On the same latitude as Naples, Italy, ie roughly 41° north and 74° west, the entire city covers a surface area of 301 sq miles (780 sq km). Of its five boroughs, only the Bronx

lies on the mainland; Manhattan and Staten Island are islands, while Brooklyn and Queens form the westernmost point of Long Island. Manhattan, the smallest borough, has a surface area of just over 22 sq miles (57 sq km), but is the most densely populated part of the city. It is 13.4 miles (21.5 km) long and between 0.8 miles (1.3 km) and 2.3 miles (3.7 km) wide.

New York lies at the mouth of the Hudson River. The East River, which borders Manhattan to the east, is not actually a river at all, but a narrow strip of water connecting Long Island Sound and Upper New York Bay.

Manhattan is laid out primarily in a rectangular system of numbered streets and avenues. An exception is the island's oldest section, from Greenwich Village south to Battery Park, an area which can be confusing without the assistance of a map.

Climate

New York is generally blessed with plenty of sunshine during all seasons of the year. High pressure areas predominate, and spells of bad weather tend to remain just that – spells. Beware, however, of the summer months of July and August: the city gets unpleasantly hot and humid, and it's hard to summon the enthusiasm to go sightseeing in temperatures of 86–102°F (30–39°C). Although New York lies on the coast, the beaches accessible by public transportation tend to be crowded, especially on hot summer weekends. The nicest beaches are half a day's trip away from Manhattan on Long Island.

Winter in New York is cold, with temperatures in January and February regularly dropping as low as 10°F

No shortage of sunshine

(–12˚C). An icy wind blows round the blocks. Snowfalls can often be heavy enough to bring traffic to a standstill, and photographs of people cross-country skiing down Fifth Avenue are not the montages they might appear.

On the other hand, May, June, September and October are very pleasant from the temperature point of view, and definitely ideal months for discovering the city.

Population

According to the 1990 census, New York City has a population of 7.3 million. Of that figure, approximately 1.5 million live in Manhattan, 2.3 million in Brooklyn, 1.9 million in Queens, 1.2 million in the Bronx and 379,000 in Staten Island. Of these, approximately 43 percent are of European descent, 25.2 percent are African-American or African-Caribbean, 6.7 percent are Asian and 24.4 percent are Latino. But New Yorkers are more than faceless numbers – they represent every race, creed and color in the world; they're the personification of 'the cultural melting pot', for which former mayor David Dinkins coined the apt, if optimistic, phrase 'gorgeous mosaic'. To walk on the sidewalks of New York is to hear Russian, Chinese, Japanese, Hindi, French, Italian, Spanish – in short, every language you can imagine (even English!)

Facing the world head on

7

Crime

No place on earth offers so many different cultures gathered in one spot; what's surprising is that, with all the city's reputation for crime, crime statistics here are actually lower than in several other large American cities. What usually catches the eye of the world, however, are lurid headlines about murders, rapes and muggings, often involving innocent or unaware out-of-towners. Obviously, it pays to be careful, use your common sense and follow a few basic safety tips (*see page 100*).

Most crime is drugs-related

Politics and administration

The city government has two major components: the mayor and the City Council. The mayor, who is elected for a four-year term, works in partnership with the council, which acts as New York's main legislative branch. As the city's official law-making body, the council monitors the operation and performance of the various city agencies. Among other tasks, it holds responsibility for analyzing and approving the city's budget. The 51 members of the council represent all five boroughs and are also elected on a four-year basis.

Economy

Contrary to the impression created by its enormous buildings, the economic life of New York City rests not only on

The New York Stock Exchange

World Financial Center

giant corporations but on the city's multitude of small businesses and factories. This diversity gives the city the flexibilty and strength to withstand hard times with less suffering than other economic centers in the US such as Detroit, with its dependence on automobile plants, and even California, supported so heavily by government contracts in the aerospace and defense industries.

New York's major industry is, as it has been for many years, apparel. Centered in Manhattan's Garment District, it still employs more than 100,000 people, and is ranked third worldwide after Paris and Los Angeles. Printing and publishing, despite the death of some newspapers in the city, continues to grow: one-third of all books published in the US are printed in New York – no other American city has more printing works. The headquarters of most of the nation's publishing houses and advertising agencies are clustered in the midtown area.

New York is also an extremely important trading center. Despite the exodus of many shipping companies to ports further from the city, the Port of New York and New Jersey remains one of the largest and most important harbors in the world. A total of 600,000 people are employed in the wholesale and retail trade.

The city sees itself as the most powerful financial center in the world. Four of the country's largest banks are based here, and the New York Stock Exchange is the largest in the world. The city's banks, real estate and insurance companies together employ at least half a million people. Other industries thriving here include management consultancies, public relations firms, architectural firms and all other businesses that gain from New York's favored status as a congress city and tourist destination. The city receives up to 25 million visitors each year – one-fifth of them from overseas.

New York has always had its financial problems, however. Today, many businesses faced with sky-high rents, are leaving the city to those who can still afford it and resettling in the neighboring suburbs. To induce expanding manufacturing companies to remain, the city has been acquiring and renting large areas of idle land in the outlying parts of Brooklyn, the Bronx, Queens and Staten Island, a program that has met with considerable success. However, the new immigrants streaming into New York are for the most part unskilled workers, many of whom find it difficult to find jobs; an additional strain has been caused by the exodus of large numbers of mainly white middle class families to the suburbs.

Despite these problems, the people and corporations behind new ideas and new products the world over are unlikely to profit all they might without the stamp of approval from New York City. Such is the depth of economic influence that, for instance, it is New York, and not Paris, that rules the wine markets and in effect determines the prices from year to year.

Outdoor activities

Media

New Yorkers are bombarded by information. People are driven by the sheer intensity of their addiction to information; in some circles it's not who you know so much as what you know. The internationally renowned *New York Times* is the paper of choice for most well-informed readers. Three tabloids compete for the rest of the audience: *New York Newsday*, the *New York Post*, famed for its garish headlines and downmarket appeal; and the *Daily News*.

The *Village Voice* is most valuable for its comprehensive listings and classified ads, while a small but feisty competitor, the *New York Press*, is one of the best of the many free weeklies to be found around town.

The three major American television networks – ABC, CBS, and NBC – broadcast many programs from their Manhattan-based studios. Free tickets are occasionally available for specific shows, but unfortunately not for the quality programs broadcast by the Public Broadcast System (PBS), also based in New York. There are three other local stations, about a dozen UHF stations, and at least four cable companies offer a wide variety viewing, from 24-hour news to 24-hour vintage movies.

Life, liberty, and the pursuit of silliness

Newspapers. Magazines. Theater. Art galleries. Museums. And, at the flick of a dial, over 100 radio and television stations. Add to this powerful corporations, award-winning modern artists, gorgeous skyscrapers, and the best music around drifting out of any number of dark, neighborhood clubs. Is it any wonder, then, that most people – locals and visitors alike – consider New York City the most vibrant place on earth?

Historical Highlights

1000 Algonquin Indian tribes use Manhattan for summer hunting and fishing.

1524 Italian maritime explorer Giovanni da Verrazano, under the patronage of Francis I of France, sights Manhattan but doesn't land.

1609 The Englishman Henry Hudson becomes the first white man to step on to the island known to the Algonquin as Mannahatta.

1624 The Dutch West India Company establishes a settlement on the southern tip of Mannahatta at the current site of Battery Park.

1626 The provincial director general of the New Amsterdam settlement, Peter Minuit, purchases Manhattan from the local Indians for 60 guilders' worth of trinkets – the equivalent of $24.

1643 Conflict with local Algonquin tribes leaves about 80 Indians dead at the Panovia Massacre.

1647 Peter Stuyvesant becomes director general. He soon suppresses all political opposition.

1653 Stuyvesant builds a fence along Wall Street to protect New Amsterdam from British incursion.

1664 In the first year of the sea war between England and Holland, Stuyvesant is forced to surrender the town to the British without a fight. New Amsterdam is renamed New York, after King Charles II's brother, James, Duke of York.

1673 The Dutch recapture New York and rename it New Orange, again without a shot being fired.

1674 New York is returned to the British as a result of the Anglo/Dutch Treaty of Westminster.

1689 James Leisler, a merchant, stages a revolt against British rule and is hanged for treason.

1690 With a population of 3,900, New York is the third-largest town in North America.

1712 Black slaves set fire to a home on Maiden Lane, hoping to incite an insurrection. Nine whites are killed. Six of the slaves commit suicide; 21 others are hanged.

1735 Newspaper publisher Peter Zenger is tried for slandering the British crown. He is acquitted, establishing the precedent for freedom of the press.

1765 In accordance with the Stamp Act, unfair taxes are levied aginst the colonists.

1770 A series of skirmishes between the Sons of Liberty and British soldiers culminate in the Battle of Golden Hill.

1776 The Revolutionary War begins and the colonies declare their independence from Great Britain. George Washington, in command of the colonial troops, loses the Battle of Long Island. British troops occupy New York until 1783.

1785 New York becomes capital of the newly-founded United States of America, but only retains this status until 1790.

1789 George Wahington is inaugurated at the site of the Federal Hall, Wall Street.

1790 A first official census reveals that New York now has a population of 33,000.

1792 The stock exchange is founded beneath a buttonwood tree on Wall Street.

1811 An important decision is made affecting the city's future appearance: all streets are to be laid out in the form of a grid.

1825 The economic importance of New York increases sharply as a result of the construction of the Erie Canal, connecting the Hudson River with the Great Lakes.

1830 Irish and German immigrants begin arriving in great numbers.

1835 The part of Manhattan between South Broad and Wall Street is ravaged by the 'Great Fire'.

1848–9 Many political refugees arrive in New York after the failure of the German Revolution.

1857 William Marcy 'Boss' Tweed, elected to the County Board of Supervisors, launches a career of notorious corruption.

1858 Calvert Vaux and Frederick Law Olmsted submit plans for the city's Central Park.

1861 The American Civil War is declared.

1863 Draft Riots rage in the city for three days. Some 1,500 people are killed.

1865 Immigration continues unabated. Italians, East European Jews and Chinese arrive in unprecedented numbers until well into the 1920s.

1871 'Boss' Tweed is arrested; later dies in jail.

1877 The Museum of Natural History opens.

1880 Metropolitan Museum of Art opens.

1883 Brooklyn Bridge officially opens. First performance is held at the Metropolitan Opera.

1886 Unveiling of the Statue of Liberty, a gift from France, on Liberty Island.

1892 Ellis Island in New York Harbor becomes the point of entry for immigrants to the US.

1898 New York's five boroughs are united under one municipal government.

1902 The Flatiron Building is completed.

1902 The Triangle Fire alerts public to the appalling work and living conditions of immigrants.

1913 Construction of the world's tallest skyscraper, the Woolworth Building. It is only superseded in 1930 by the Chrysler Building.

1929 The Wall Street Crash, and the start of the Great Depression in the USA and worldwide.

1931 The Empire State Building opens.

1933–45 Many Europeans take refuge in New York from ethnic and political persecution at the hands of the German Nazi regime.

1939 Ten years after its foundation by Abby Aldrich Rockefeller, the Museum of Modern Art moves into its new home on 53rd Street.

1941 United States enters World War II.

1943 Serious racial unrest in Harlem, which has been an important African-American community since 1910.

1946 New York becomes the seat of the United Nations Organization (UNO), founded the previous year.

1959 The Guggenheim Museum, designed by Frank Lloyd Wright, opens its doors for the first time. Work begins on the Lincoln Center

1965 A 16-hour-long power cut brings the city to a standstill.

1970 Economic decline sets in as firms start leaving the city in ever-increasing numbers. This decline continues until around 1976.

1973 World Trade Center opens.

1975 The city's chronic financial situation reaches its peak: bankruptcy is only avoided via a bridging loan from the federal government.

1977 A second major power cut, this time 27 hours long. Looting and vandalism.

1980 Ex-Beatle John Lennon is shot dead outside the Dakota Building on Central Park.

1982 IBM Building opens, followed by the AT&T Building in 1983, affirming the resurgence of corporate development.

1983 Trump Tower, a vast glass complex of shops, offices and apartments on Fifth Avenue, is completed. It symbolizes the gradual emergence of economic stagnation.

1902 Battery Park City opens.

1987 'Black Monday' on Wall Street. Shares suffer a sudden 30 percent drop in value.

1990 David Dinkins becomes the city's first ever African-American mayor.

1993 Bomb explodes below World Trade Center. Many are injured.

1994 Rudolph Giuliani becomes mayor of New York in succession to David Dinkins.

ROUTES 1 & 2
LOWER MANHATTAN

Ⓢ Subway

0 ———————— 0.25 miles

LITTLE ITALY

CHINA

TRIBECA

BATTERY PARK CITY

LOWER MANHATTAN

FINANCIAL DISTRICT

Hudson River

Police Headquarters

Civic Center

World Trade Center

Meryll Lynch

American Express

Dow Jones

Battery Park

Statue of Liberty, Ellis Island

Staten Island

Delancey Street

Broome Street

Street

Street

S

Grand Street

Norfolk St.

②

LOWER EAST SIDE

Elizabeth St.

Bowery

Chrystie Street

Forsyth Street

Eldridge

Allen

Orchard St.

Essex Street

Hester Street

Canal Street

TOWN

E. Broadway

Street Market

Pike

Henry Street

Madison Street

Street

Henry Street

Catherine

Madison St.

Monroe Street

St.

St.

Cherry Street

Street

Highway

South Elevated

Wagner Pl.

River

St.

Brooklyn Bridge

South Street Seaport

East

Furman Street

Brooklyn Queens Expwy.

Columbia Heights

N

VISTA

Route 1

★★ World Trade Center – ★Battery Park City –
★★★ Statue of Liberty and Ellis Island – ★Financial
District – ★ South Street Seaport

Lower Manhattan is the original New York, where winding streets once led to bustling docks and clipper ships. Today these narrow byways, with names like Pine Street, Pearl Street and Wall Street, are lined by towering temples of finance. If you want to see the sights from the inside as well as the outside, it's best to plan two to three days for Route 1; otherwise the whole route can also be done on foot within a day. *See map, pages 14/15.*

The World Trade Center

A plaza measuring 24,000sq yds (20,000sq m), the largest enclosed shopping area in New York, with 208 elevators, 50,000 jobs, 80,000 visitors daily and two 1,377ft (420m) high towers – even for this city of superlatives, it's utterly gigantic. The ★★ **World Trade Center** ❶ can no longer lay claim to being the world's tallest building, though it was for a few months in 1973, just after its completion. That same year Chicago set new standards with its Sears Tower (1,453ft/443m).

The most famous restaurant in the Trade Center is at the top of Tower 1 (North Tower): **Windows on the World**. Only the smartly-dressed (jacket and tie) are allowed in, and the prices are nearly as high as the establishment itself. The view of New York is stunning from here, though there's also a far cheaper way of enjoying it: an elevator takes just 58 seconds to get to the enclosed observation deck on the 107th floor of Tower 2 (South Tower). The very brave – with a head for heights – could even try the rooftop promenade on the 110th floor (only open on clear, calm days). However fast the ride up is, though, be prepared for long delays in summertime because of the crush of visitors. On gloomy days it's also a good idea to check whether it's worth making an ascent at all: a display in the foyer provides information on daily visibility. By the way, a tip if you are a theater lover: a TKTS office is located in Tower 2 (*see page 83*).

*The observation deck
is on the 107th floor*

From the technical point of view the construction of the twin towers was a magnificent achievement. Because of the sheer height involved, the building had to be assembled from the inside out: cranes installed in the lift-shafts hoisted tons of steel, and gradually built the outer walls. The building's aesthetic value remains controversial, however, and critics accused design architect Minoru Yamasaki of creating too bare and massive a structure.

The complex known as ★**Battery Park City**, overlooking the Hudson River, actually owes its existence to the

The Esplanade in Battery Park City

World Trade Center – it was built on top of the landfill that remained after its construction. The new land became state property and construction work was carried out according to a harmonious urban plan.

The commercial center of the complex is the ★ **World Financial Center ❷**, which is reached from the World Trade Center via a glass bridge (North Bridge). The four stocky towers containing offices have a remarkably cozy air to them in contrast to the Twin Towers of the World Trade Center, and the squares, shopping arcades and public-access lobbies are all far more successful from the design point of view. The atmosphere here is pleasant, with music playing, people strolling, dining; marble and brass fittings add a note of majesty, and palm trees in the conservatory lend a tropical flair. Creating space accessible to everyone was one of the main objectives of the city planners; 30 percent of the area covered by Battery Park City fulfills this stipulation. The Esplanade is one of the most popular parks here, probably because it is one of the city's few scenic walkways along the water's edge. Another is the new Hudson River Park just to the north of the World Financial Center, which has given nearby residents a much-needed river view of their own.

South Bridge, the southern connection between the World Financial and World Trade Centers, leads to Liberty Street. Beyond it is Broadway, which leads south to three buildings of note: the **U.S. Realty Building** (115 Broadway), the **Trinity Building** (111 Broadway), both of them elegant skyscrapers dating from 1906, and the **Equitable Building ❸** opposite. A massive structure dating from 1915, it caused such a stir when built that new zoning ordinances were introduced a year later, designed to prevent city streets from becoming sunless canyons and leading to the introduction of stepped skyscrapers.

World Financial Center – a pleasant atmosphere

The Equitable Building

The diminutive Trinity Church

Trinity tomb

Some like it hot: Bowling Green

Once upon a time, church towers rather than huge office blocks dominated the landscape. Today, nestling between the many temples of wealth around it, the red-sandstone **Trinity Church ❹** is a relic of that era. The first church was built on this site in 1697, but burnt down in 1776, the year of the Declaration of Independence, during which the British began their siege of New York by reducing much of it to rubble. A second structure was built in 1790, but was torn down in 1839 and replaced with the present, newly-scrubbed neo-Gothic one. The church interior is simple and unpretentious; the bronze doors were added in the 20th century. The churchyard dates from 1681, and contains the pyramid-shaped tomb of Alexander Hamilton, first secretary of the US Treasury.

Trinity Church marks the first stage of a journey back in time. Further south, where Broadway crosses Exchange Place, is the presumed site of the camp of the Dutch explorer Captain Adriaen Block and his crew, who arrived here in 1614, six years before the Pilgrims landed on Plymouth Rock. They didn't intend to stay at all, but their ship burned, forcing them to remain on Manhattan Island for the winter while they built a new seagoing vessel – appropriately named *Restless*.

The next Europeans to arrive were eager to stay, however. Dutch colonists settled on the island of *Mannahatta* – as the Indians called it – in 1624, and in 1626 Peter Minuit, director general of the Dutch Province of New Netherland, 'purchased' Manhattan from the Indians for 60 guilders ($24) worth of trinkets. This dubious transaction is said to have taken place in the fenced pocket park known today as **Bowling Green ❺**. In the early days of the city, Bowling Green was a market-place, and was also used for troop exercises; later on, though, during the struggle for independence from Britain, it developed into

a center of resistance. Tensions were so high during the 1770s that a statue of the English king, George III, erected on the green in 1770, had to be protected just one year later from the angry crowds by a fence. In 1776, after the adoption of the Declaration of Independence, both statue and fence swiftly fell victim to popular sentiment.

Bowling Green: bull statue

To the north of Bowling Green is a building with a very fine lobby: the **Cunard Building** ❻ (25 Broadway); it was built in 1921 to house the headquarters of the famous Cunard shipping line.

The southern side of the green is dominated by the former **US Custom House** ❼, a fine Beaux-Arts building completed in 1907. Cass Gilbert was the architect; the four sculptures representing Asia, America, Europe and Africa are by Daniel Chester French. The 12 statues along the sixth-floor cornice symbolize historical trading centers: Greece, Rome, Phoenicia, Genoa, Venice, Spain, Holland, Portugal, Denmark, Germany, England and France. (Anti-German sentiment in 1917 caused the statue for Germany to be renamed 'Belgium'.) In late 1994, the Custom House became the **George Gustav Heye Center of the National Museum of the American Indian**. The newly renovated interior is now filled with a fascinating selection of Native American artwork and crafts with religious or social significance, part of a collection of artefacts until recently located in a museum in the northern part of Manhattan. Admission is free.

US Custom House

19

A fortress stood on the site of the Custom House for 150 years. It was built by the Dutch, but they could not muster enough men to defend it and in 1664 the town and its fortifications fell to the British without a fight. Fort James, or Fort George as it was later called, was used by the British until the adoption of the Declaration of Independence, when it was finally pulled down. A Government house was built on its site and a president was supposed to move into it – New York was the country's capital from 1785 to 1790. In 1811, when England and France were at war, fortified defenses seemed necessary once more: England was threatening the young US nation, hoping to deter it from trading with the French.

Just to the south (across State Street) is Battery Park, where another fortress was built: originally called the West Battery, today it's known appropriately as **Castle Clinton** ❽ (after an early New York City mayor, not the president), and in 1824, it was converted into a place of entertainment and renamed Castle Garden. During the first half of the 19th century concerts and festivals of all kinds were held here; it was here in 1850 that Jenny Lind, brought over from Sweden by the famous manager-impresario PT Barnum, made her debut in front of a crowd of 6,000 people. Five years later, though, Castle Garden was in use

War Memorial in Battery Park

as an immigrant processing center. Things began to look up for Castle Garden in 1896, when the popular New York Aquarium moved in. The old walls were saved from demolition in the 1940s, and the semi-circular fortress became a national monument.

All aboard for Liberty Island

Walk through Battery Park to **South Ferry** ❾, where the ferries to both Ellis Island and **Liberty Island** dock. Tickets for both ferries are sold inside Castle Clinton, and the ferry to the latter runs daily between 9am and 4pm (departure on the hour, and every half-hour in summertime). The ★★★ **Statue of Liberty** is even more popular since the celebration of its centenary in 1986. The ferry trip lasts just 20 minutes, but there's waiting around once you get to the island: for the elevator inside that takes you half way up, and then for the flight of 168 steps leading to the crown (after 2pm, there's no guarantee of making it to the very top).

Ms Liberty mementos

The statue is 46m/151ft high, but its pedestal is nearly the same height; indeed, the history of the pedestal is perhaps even more interesting than that of the statue itself. *Liberty Enlightening the World* – was donated to America by the French as an expression of their admiration for the American Revolution, which they termed 'the completion of the French Revolution across the Atlantic.' The original proposal was made by the historian Edouard de Laboulaye; the sculptor responsible was Frédéric-Auguste Bartholdi; and Gustave Eiffel constructed the scaffolding inside.

Ms Liberty crossed the Atlantic in 200 packing cases, and arrived in New York Harbor in 1885. But there was a problem: the French had made it a condition that the New Yorkers build a suitable pedestal for their generous present. The fact that this was almost as expensive as the statue dampened the enthusiasm of many wealthy New Yorkers, who saw no point in paying indirectly for a present that had been forced on them.

The Statue of Liberty arrived in 1885

Which explains why $100,000 for the pedestal were still missing when the crates containing the famous lady arrived in New York Harbor – until a man named Joseph Pulitzer saved the day. A prominent publisher (for whom the Pulitzer Prize is named), he organized a campaign for donations in his newspaper *The World*, promising that all benefactors would be mentioned by name. It turned out to be a clever move: within six months he had not only collected the required sum, but also significantly increased the circulation of his newspaper.

Liberty Enlightening the World was unveiled with much pomp on October 28, 1886. Then something strange happened. It may have had something to do with the site chosen for the statue – so exposed right out in the harbor, so high above the ocean and the masts of the ships – or perhaps the pose, with the arm outstretched as if in greeting. Whatever the reason, within just a few years the statue's original significance was forgotten and what the French saw as a symbol of Franco-American brotherhood was soon regarded as the incarnation of American freedom. *Liberty Enlightening the World* became the 'Mother of Exiles,' greeting all the immigrants with the words carved into a plaque at the entrance to her pedestal:

'Give me your tired, your poor,
  Your huddled masses yearning to breathe free,
  The wretched refuse of your teeming shore.
  Send these, the homeless, the tempest-tost to me,
  I lift my lamp beside the golden door!'

Over 16 million immigrants traveled through that open door between 1892 and 1954; the **Statue of Liberty Museum**, situated on the first floor of the pedestal, is dedicated to them.

From 1898 to 1924, the route taken by the new arrivals first led them to ★★ **Ellis Island**, a small dot in the harbor where immigrants were asked embarrassing questions and searched. The 'tempest-tost' dreaded this humiliating inspection, for the reality of immigration was very different from the poetic promise. Laws, which were changed according to the current political situation and the number of immigrants arriving, barred the sick, the weak, the politically undesirable, the penniless and even unmarried women from entering the land of the free. Those who failed the test were detained on the island and sent back on the next available ship – a cruel end to all those dreams of a bright new future.

Two thousand immigrants a day was no rarity during the record years of 1907 and 1914. And when one imagines what conditions must have been like in the Great Hall of the main building, 'huddled masses yearning to breathe free' takes on a different connotation entirely. Restoration work was completed on the island's buildings in 1990, and the exhibits are as wrenching as they are fascinating.

Apart from the ferries to Liberty and Ellis islands, visitors should consider taking the **Staten Island Ferry** ❿, which docks east of the US Coastguard Building. On its way to the borough of Staten Island it crosses New York Harbor. The ★★ **view** of the Statue of Liberty and the Manhattan skyline is superb, and costs just 50 cents.

From Battery Park, continue northwards via State Street – where No 7 still exudes the wealth and elegance of early 19th-century New York – to Whitehall Street, and then up Pearl Street. A 19th-century block on the corner of Pearl

Ellis Island and the Great Hall

A great view for 50 cents

Interior of Fraunces Tavern

Coenties Slip

Hanover Square statue

Street and Broad Street contains the **Fraunces Tavern** ⓫, named after Samuel Fraunces who ran it from 1762. When the English took New York in 1776, Fraunces became George Washington's steward, and on December 4, 1783 the general returned here for lunch and bade farewell to his troops.

The present structure dates from 1907 and is an approximation of the original tavern which was built in 1719. The museum on the upper storeys contains historical documents and period furniture. The ground floor is still a restaurant, frequented these days not by revolutionaries but by bankers and stockbrokers working in the Financial District.

Before entering the world of Mammon, take a short detour east to the harbor and to **Coenties Slip**. A *slip* was an old docking bay for merchant ships, and several street-names still contain the word. Much of the southern tip of Manhattan was formerly water: the area east of Pearl Street is all reclaimed land. The ★ **Vietnam Veterans Memorial** ⓬ here is a simple wall of green glass showing extracts from soldiers' letters – senselessness of war and the desperation of those forced to take part has rarely been more eloquently conveyed.

The route now follows Water Street northwards and then bears left to attractive little **Hanover Square** ⓭, which derives its name from the time of the monarchy (George I was from the House of Hanover). While some wonder why its name wasn't changed under the young Republic, Hanover Square was a fine address, and in the course of the 18th century developed into the center of New York business. However, due to the great fire of 1835, which broke out on the corner of Hanover Square and Pearl Street and destroyed most of the area flanked by South, Broad and Wall Street, not a single original structure survives: over 600 buildings burned down during those three terrible winter days; the extreme cold made it almost impossible to extinguish the flames because the water froze in the hoses.

The finest building in Hanover Square, **India House**, dates from the period of reconstruction. Built between 1851 and 1854 it originally served as a bank building and today houses an overseas trading club. On the ground floor is **Harry's** restaurant, something of an institution in Wall Street banking and stockbroking circles. Its big rival is **Delmonico's**, at 56 Beaver Street. Insiders can work out which of the two contains the more successful clientele; outsiders are left hoping the business transacted in both restaurants is more successful than what's served at the tables. True Wall Street tycoons don't seem to mind all that much, though. Long before their minions have arrived at the office in the morning they'll already be making decisions over a 'power breakfast' of muesli and orange juice. These take place between 7 and 9am and – if you're lucky enough to get a table at either Harry's or Delmonico's – can be a good way of soaking up the legendary Wall Street atmosphere.

★ **Wall Street** is best observed at its most hectic time of day: shortly before 9am on weekdays. Limousines with tinted glass, women in business suits wearing sneakers, smart young brokers wearing Walkmen are everywhere. Thousands of them pour out of subways and vanish through the revolving doors of banks and office buildings – and then suddenly everything is quite still, and Wall Street seems almost deserted.

The street dates back to the very early days of the city and is named after an earthen wall built to protect the Dutch settlement. When the English arrived in 1664 the wall turned out to be as effective from the defensive point of view as the unmanned fort near Bowling Green. The conquerors pulled the wall down quite quickly after that, and the city spread northwards; a slave market was installed at the center of today's Financial District, and later on it became a grain market.

The seeds of Wall Street's future fame were sown in 1792. Newly-formed New York State was in severe financial difficulties as a result of the struggle for independence, and decided to issue bonds. To discuss conditions of trade, 24 brokers met beneath a buttonwood tree on Wall Street and founded the New York Stock Exchange. That same year they moved into the rooms of the Tontine Coffee House on the corner of Wall Street and Water Street, before building the Stock Exchange on today's site at 20 Broad Street. Wall Street remains a traditional locale for deal-clinching, though, and the sign-language used by

Wall Street wealth
The morning rush is over

23

A break from the floor

today's brokers is supposed to date back to the time when partners in adjoining buildings had to be informed about buying and selling from the sidewalk below.

By the end of the 19th century, the industrial revolution had changed the face of the world, and some people had grown inordinately rich as a result of the American Civil War. Small businesses were passé and huge corporations began to form, most with a need for more money than they actually had at their disposal. The banks soon found the necessary capital and trade in securities reached record levels. Wall Street prospered. But on October 29, 1929, the day that came to be known as 'Black Friday', the bubble burst. The stock market dramatically collapsed, ushering in a global slump. Stories of bankrupt shareholders committing suicide by jumping out of skyscrapers went round the world.

Today's reports about corruption, artificially inflated share prices and other semi-legal activities continue to provide Hollywood with much exciting material. Methods have changed on Wall Street over the past 20 years, though, and competition is tougher than ever: the real estate firms have become corporations now, and brokers' commissions can be freely negotiated.

Walking along Wall Street in the direction of Trinity Church, take a look inside the early-19th-century lobby of Citibank at No 55. At No 23 is the **Morgan Guaranty Trust Company Building**. At the turn of the century, JP Morgan was the wealthiest and most influential banker in the world. The building was completed in 1914, and a bomb went off outside it in 1920 – traces of the blast can still be seen on the walls.

Seen from the outside, the ★ **New York Stock Exchange** ⑭ looks very much like a temple, with its huge pillars and elaborate frieze on the portico. It was built in

Stock Exchange messengers

Stock Exchange – the main floor

1903 and enlarged in 1923. The entrance to the Visitor Center is at 20 Broad Street (Monday to Friday, 9.15am–4pm); guards direct visitors to elevators that take them up to a gallery overlooking the main floor. Here, a number of interactive machines and displays attempt to shed some light on the different activities of the gentlemen in baggy suits downstairs.

The temple-like exterior

There are more interactive video terminals opposite the New York Stock Exchange in **Federal Hall** , a magnificent neoclassical building on the corner of Wall Street and Nassau Street. The site was previously occupied by New York's old city hall, built around 1701, the scene of a trial that became a milestone in the history of press freedom. In 1735, John Peter Zenger, publisher of the *New York Weekly Journal*, was arrested for libel after allowing the publication of several articles in his paper accusing British colonial governor William Cosby of corruption. To the delight of the general public, the colonial jury acquitted Zenger on the grounds that his charges were based on fact – a key consideration in libel cases since that time.

Federal Hall

Another announcement – made on this site 41 years after the trial took place – was just as unwelcome to the colonial government:

'We hold these truths to be self-evident, that all men are created equal, that they are endowed by their Creator with certain unalienable Rights, that among these are Life, Liberty and the pursuit of Happiness. That to secure these rights, Governments are instituted among Men, deriving their just powers from the consent of the governed. That whenever any Form of Government becomes destructive of these ends, it is the Right of the People to alter or to abolish it…'

Powerful words, which were translated into action 13 years before the French Revolution. They occur at the beginning of the Declaration of Independence that was approved and signed in Philadelphia on July 4, 1776 by the Second Continental Congress. The only colony that did not sign was New York, but that didn't prevent the rebels from reading out the document outside the old city hall 14 days later.

There was still a long way to go between declaring independence to creating a fully-functioning state: a common constitution was finally agreed upon in 1787. In 1789, the first president was appointed: George Washington, whose statue stands outside Federal Hall. It was in his honor that the old city hall was renovated and had its name changed: for just over a year it served as the Capitol.

After New York had ceased to be the nation's capital, the old city hall fell into disrepair and was pulled down. Today's structure dates from 1842 and was originally the City Custom House. The museum inside is open week-

25

days, and serves as a reminder of the momentous events that took place here in the past.

On the other side of Federal Hall is Pine Street. Follow this, keeping to the right, and soon **Chase Manhattan Plaza**  comes into view, with its interesting *Four Trees* sculpture by Jean Dubuffet. Cross the broad, windy square and then follow Nassau Street northwards. Liberty Street on the left (on the corner of Liberty Place) contains a marvelous Beaux Arts building dating from 1901, one which housed the Chamber of Commerce of the State of New York until 1980.

Chase Manhattan Plaza

Keen on money? The building that takes up the entire block between Maiden Lane, Nassau and Liberty is the **Federal Reserve Bank** ⓱. Its resemblance to the Palazzo Strozzi in Florence is intentional. Designed by architects York & Sawyer, it was completed in 1924, and its fortress-like appearance has a purpose: the building's underground vaults are rumoured to contain more gold than Fort Knox. The building's entrance lobby on Liberty Street is suitably impressive. (Tours are available on weekdays.)

Passing Louise Nevelson Plaza – named after the New York artist whose abstract sculptures it contains – the route now goes eastwards along Maiden Lane as far as Front Street. Keep left along it as far as Fulton Street and the ★ **South Street Seaport**. This area of the city is quite a mixture: it's a museum (with exhibitions on New York's maritime history, old ships, workshops, etc), a shopping center (with boutiques, gift shops and galleries in the old houses and the Pier 17 Pavilion), a starting-point for round harbor trips, a fine place to eat and a center of entertainment. A variety of open-air events are held here in the summer, spring and fall.

South Street Seaport

New York owes its rise to prominence as a world capital to this harbor. It was here that overseas trade first

The historic ships – the big attraction at piers 15 and 16

began, and where the large sailing ships from all over the world used to dock. However, the arrival of the steamship in the mid-19th century ushered in a period of steady decline, for there was more room for piers along the Hudson River. The area on the East Side thus fell into disrepair.

It was eventually awoken from its long sleep by a revitalization program begun in 1967. An alliance was formed with commercial interests to underwrite restoration of the old harbor buildings and a growing collection of antique sailing vessels.

The area around South Street was always busy: the streets were filled with seamen and traders; the brownstone houses along John, Fulton, Beekman and Peck Streets contained bars, brothels and cheap boarding houses; markets were held in the squares; and chandlers, sailmakers, ropemakers and other craftsmen who relied on the harbor for their livelihood all had shops in the narrow houses here. Turning the place into a silent museum would not have done justice to the harbor atmosphere that existed in the 19th century.

Schermerhorn Row

The historic district of South Street Seaport is made up of 12 blocks of early 19th-century buildings and three piers. **Schermerhorn Row** ⓲, on the south side of Fulton Street, consists of a series of commercial buildings in the Georgian-Federal and Greek Revival style. The Museum Visitors Center, where maps as well as tickets for the museum and boat tours can be obtained, is located at 12 Fulton Street. There is also a ticket office at Pier 16. The big attraction of this museum are the historic ships at Piers 15 and 16, which include the classic square-rigger *Wavertree* (1885), the ferryboat *Major-General William H Hart* (1925), the four-masted *Peking* (1911) and the lightship *Ambrose* (1906).

The harbor trips organized by Seaport Liberty Cruises (tel: 212-630 8888) take 1½ hours to go round the southern tip of Manhattan, with views of the Statue of Liberty, Ellis Island, the World Trade Center and Battery Park.

From Pier 17, with its popular shops and restaurants, you can obtain an excellent view of the ★★ **Brooklyn Bridge.** This masterpiece of 19th-century bridge-building was designed by John Roebling. After his death during the first year of construction (he contracted tetanus after his foot was crushed by a docking ferry) his son Washington took over. Rising too fast from an underwater chamber, he suffered an attack of the bends and was wheelchair-bound from then on. Nevertheless, he and his wife oversaw the project to its conclusion, and the bridge was finally opened in May 1883. The best way to experience it is on foot; the entrance to the pedestrian walkway is at the ends of Frankfort Street and Park Row, both a few blocks further north.

The Brooklyn Bridge

St Paul's Chapel

FW Woolworth counting coins and the exterior of his building

Route 2

★★ World Trade Center – St Paul's Chapel – City Hall Park – Foley Square – ★★ Chinatown – ★ Little Italy – Lower East Side

The area south of East Houston Street, on the Lower East Side, is another part of the city that deserves a full day to explore – if not longer. *See map, pages 14/15.*

The starting-point of this route is the ★★ **World Trade Center** again, for two reasons: first, it's the ideal subway stop and second, its two gigantic towers provide a wonderful contrast to **St Paul's Chapel** ⑲, situated on the corner of Broadway and Fulton Street. This is where the Old World meets the New: St Paul's is quintessentially European. Its architect, Thomas McBean, was probably a pupil of James Gibbs, who built St-Martin-in-the-Fields in London. The chapel was completed in 1766, and is authentic Georgian apart from the steeple, which was added 30 years later. It has two claims to fame: it is both the oldest church as well as the oldest civic building in Manhattan. George Washington worshipped here – his private pew in the north aisle is marked with a 'G'. The little churchyard is an oasis of peace.

Vesey Street passes to the north of the square outside the church, and two buildings on it merit closer inspection: the **Garrison Building** (No 20), built in 1906, with its interesting triple facade, and the **New York County Lawyers' Association Building** (No 14), erected by Cass Gilbert in 1930. It is one of his less complex structures when compared with the US Custom House on Bowling Green (*see page 18*) and the **Woolworth Building** ⑳. This flamboyant 'Cathedral of Commerce,' which made Gilbert world-famous, is a block further north on Broadway, between Barclay Street and Park Place, and is considered by many to be the finest commercial building in the world. Frank Winfield Woolworth, the farm worker turned shop assistant and then retail entrepreneur, had this neo-Gothic temple built in honor of himself, his stores and his success story. By the time he died in 1919, his company controlled over 1,000 stores from its New York headquarters. The three-story-high entrance hall with its beautiful mosaic ceiling contains statues of Gilbert and Woolworth, the former holding a model of the building, the latter shown counting coins.

With its 66 stories, the Woolworth Building had the additional distinction of being the tallest in the world (not counting the Eiffel Tower) for 18 years, from its construction in 1912 to 1930. Its 790ft (241m) were then superseded by the 1,043ft (318m) of the Chrysler Building

City Hall Park

(*see page 54*), which was beaten yet again by the Empire State Building (1,250ft/381m) (*see page 45*) just one year later. At this stage it was clear how the focal point of the business world had shifted within the city, from downtown to midtown.

During the 18th century, when only the southern tip of Manhattan island was inhabited, the area between Broadway, Park Row and Chambers Street, known today as **City Hall Park** , was still a common. 'Commons' and 'greens' were an English export, and are still found at the center of most New England villages. The open area of lawn formed an integral part of every settlement, and was used as grazing land or for military exercises and meetings. Public buildings such as prisons and almshouses were also situated here, as were the gallows.

When New York began to expand northwards at the beginning of the 19th century, and its inhabitants needed a new town hall – the third in just 170 years – they chose the common as a construction site. The architects' competition for the new **City Hall** was won by Joseph F Mangin and John McComb, a Frenchman and a Scotsman, and each added elements from their respective homelands: the building is a mixture of French Renaissance and English Georgian. It was officially opened in 1812, with a fine marble facade to the south and ordinary-looking brownstone (for reasons of economy) to the north. The fact that the building still fulfills its original function as official seat of the mayor and the City Council (plus museum) is a wonder, considering the rate at which New York used up its city halls in colonial times. This magnificent building was threatened with closure and demolition on several occasions during its history. In 1956 the decision was finally made to thoroughly restore it and thus preserve one of the finest historic structures in the United States. The original marble facade was refaced with Alabama sandstone.

29

City Hall was opened in 1812

Hall of Records: facade detail

Behind it stands the former **New York County Courthouse** ㉒, dubbed the 'Tweed' courthouse on its completion in 1878 after the scandalous revelation that 'Boss' Tweed, the notorious fraudster and Democratic party boss who died that same year, had lined his own pockets with around $9 million of its final cost.

A short walk away from the Tweed Courthouse is the former **AT Stewart Dry-Goods Store** ㉓, on the corner of Broadway and Chambers Street. AT Stewart was a successful businessman, and the textile and sundries outlet he opened here in 1846 was the first department store in New York. The building was purchased by the *New York Sun* in 1917, and the attractive clock dates from its heyday.

The building with the twin towers, next door, was built for a bank in 1908. Today it is civic property, as is the **Hall of Records** ㉔, which was completed in 1911 and is one of the finest Beaux Arts buildings in New York. The facade, dominated by eight Corinthian columns, and several sculpture groups and statues, hides a rather sober interior: the building also contains the Surrogate's Court.

At the eastern end of Chambers Street is the **Municipal Building** ㉕, which dates from 1914. Despite the massive size of this structure, the team of architects who designed it – McKim, Mead and White – managed to fashion an impressive contrast to City Hall.

Chambers Street disappears under the Municipal Building and ends up beyond it in Police Plaza – named after Police Headquarters, which is situated to the east of it. Park Row, formerly known as 'Newspaper Row,' connects here from the south: between 1840 and the turn of the century this street contained the headquarters of every major paper in the city. Northwards up Centre Street is **Foley Square** ㉖. The row of administrative and judicial buildings belonging to the Civic Center continues here, with the two modern structures making up the **Jacob K Javits Federal Building** (1967 and 1976), the **New York County Courthouse** (1926), and the **US Courthouse** (1936). Other buildings along Centre Street include the New York City Department of Health and the nondescript Civil Courthouse – in short, government and administration buildings everywhere you look. At the junction of Centre and White Streets it's worth making a short detour to the left: on the corner of Lafayette and White is what looks like a French château but was built in 1895 as a **fire station**.

Follow White Street as far as Baxter Street, turn down Bayard and suddenly you're in another world. The telephone booths have pagoda roofs, the shop signs are all written in Chinese, and shopkeepers can be seen carrying crates and boxes full of exotic vegetables and spices. Red ducks dangle from shop windows, and a few steps

The fire station

A winning hand
The bustle of Chinatown

further on shops sell satin shoes, jade, kimonos, kites and cricket cages. This is New York's famous ★★ **Chinatown**. It has been estimated that this section of the city is home to 70–80,000 people, and the population is increasing all the time. Most residents are from Taiwan and Hong Kong; indeed, the latter's uncertain future has prompted many to invest in New York. Chinatown has now spread well beyond its original borders of Bowery, Baxter, Canal and Worth streets and gradually made inroads into neighboring Little Italy and the Lower East Side.

Life in Chinatown is a rule unto itself. The singsong voices, the innumerable, overladen fruit and vegetable stalls, the lack of spoken English – it's like being in an entirely different country. The towers of the World Trade Center and the Empire State in the distance are the only reminders that this is actually still New York and not Taipei or Canton.

Assuming there isn't a festival on – Chinese New Year, for instance, held in January or February – New Yorkers generally visit Chinatown to eat. There are hundreds of small, unpretentious restaurants here, all serving up magnificent delicacies. More often than not they are cramped, noisy and a bit shabby, and tables can't usually be reserved: sometimes lines form outside the most popular establishments on Saturdays and Sunday mornings, when the New Yorkers make their weekend pilgrimages here for a delicious *dim-sum* brunch. (*Dim-sum* is a collection of tasty steamed delicacies trundled through the restaurant on a trolley; diners take as much as they like, and pay according to the number and type of plates they choose.) Among the most popular restaurants are: **Nice Restaurant** (35 East Broadway), **Hee Seung Fung** (46 Bowery), and **Silver Palace** (50 Bowery). As far as the other restaurants are concerned, each New Yorker has his or her favorite, and it's best to try them out yourself.

Mulberry Street in Little Italy

Welcoming staff

Pizza and pasta delights

For coffee or dessert take a short walk across Canal Street back to Europe: ★ **Little Italy** has a fine selection of typical Italian food and espresso – but can be a bit on the expensive side. A slice of cake in Little Italy can often cost as much as a full meal in Chinatown. **Mulberry Street** is lined with restaurants, cafes, delicatessens and small houses with zigzag fire escapes, which give the neighborhood a certain European flair.

In mid-September, when Mulberry Street gets decked out in honor of the Feast of San Gennaro, Little Italy turns into a huge block party, with food stalls, processions and thousands of people. Along with the equally boisterous Feast of St Anthony in June, it's a New York experience not to be missed.

Not far away, an apartment in the former **NYC Police Headquarters ㉗** – which takes up the entire block between Grand, Center and Broome Streets and Center Market Place – can cost up to $1.8 million. This French Renaissance style palazzo dating from 1909 is a reminder that Little Italy is no longer just an area for immigrants (just as Chinatown is spreading north and east, the well-heeled populace of SoHo marches south.)

A few blocks east is the **Bowery**, one of New York's more notorious streets. If Fifth Avenue was synonymous with wealth and success, the Bowery was associated for decades with social deprivation and alcoholism. The street was distinctive for its vagrants, bars and cheap boarding-houses – there were four or five bars per block here as recently as the 1940s and 50s.

Although today the Bowery boasts shops, rock clubs (CBGB being the oldest and best known), even a few trendy restaurants, it's still pretty seedy. One notable cultural exception – redolent of a period in the 19th century, when this was a thriving theater district – is the **Bouverie Lane Theatre**; another is the tiny, family-run **Amato Opera Theater**, on the corner of 2nd Street.

The Bouverie Lane Theatre

Before it went into decline at the end of the 19th century, the Bowery was a very fine street. The Dutch governor Peter Stuyvesant used it as an approach road for his country estate of *Bouwerij*, and anyone headed northwards in the direction of Boston would gallop along it. During the second half of the 19th century the street developed a slight – but only very slight – notoriety when the Germans made it their entertainment district. The street not only contained several beer-halls, but also theaters, music halls and glee clubs.

Unlike some other ethnic groups – eg the Irish, who left their land for purely economic reasons – the Germans who settled the **Lower East Side** during the 19th century were mostly middle-class, and had emigrated for predominantly political reasons. They were also largely Protestant, and having the same religion as the group entrenched in power was one reason why they faced fewer difficulties in their new home than, say, the Irish, who often had to put up with intense anti-Catholic feeling.

Many of the politically active liberals who emigrated in their thousands after the failure of the German Revolution of 1848 settled the area between Bowery, East River, Grand Street and 14th Street. 'Little Germany' became a small city in its own right, with all the corresponding cultural and social institutions: libraries, theaters, churches and hospitals. There were German newspapers of varying political persuasions, and the Germans of the Lower East Side also contributed a great deal to the American Labor and Trade Union Movements. From 1880 onwards, however, the German community on the Lower East Side began to dissolve: Little Germany shifted northwards to the former village of Yorkville (on today's Upper east Side of Manhattan), which was now connected by public transport and had become part of the city.

The area began to fill up with a massive new wave of immigrants fleeing Europe: after the assassination of Tsar Alexander II in 1881, and the ensuing programs, there began a mass emigration of Russian and East European Jews. In the following decades, more than 2 million of them came to the United States, and over 500,000 settled in New York City, mostly on the Lower East Side. Grand Street, between Broadway and Essex Street, was the main shopping street in the city at that time, and textile wholesalers and suppliers had their warehouses along Canal Street. The area filled with garment trade sweatshops, kosher restaurants and synagogues, and by 1900

33

the Lower East Side had become the most densely populated urban area in the world.

This was the new world ghetto, where the 'needle trade' was the cornerstone of the economy. Tenement rooms were often cluttered with piles of half-sewn clothes on the floor. Payment was made on a piecework basis. The working conditions were appalling and the wages pitiful. The Hester Street market was the focal point of the neighborhood, and of those Jews who did not enter the needle trade many worked as peddlers or pushcart vendors selling meats, fish, produce or cheap clothing.

But the Jews soon established their presence, organizing themselves into unions and advocating immigrant rights through their various newspapers. Cultural and religious traditions were maintained. Day after day the people of the Lower East Side ground out a living – working, saving, moving slowly ahead – and created a niche for themselves in the complex cultural and economic world of New York City. The Jews who made their fortunes here have long since moved further north or across to Brooklyn, but ★ **Orchard Street** still gives an impression of what it must have been like to live here during those early days: small, cramped shops containing heaps of socks, underwear and jeans; amazing discounts that become even more attractive after a bit of haggling. Avoid the area on Friday or Saturday though: many shopowners are Orthodox and most shops are closed.

Instead, pay a visit to the ★ **Lower East Side Tenement Museum**, which opened in 1988 and includes an almost perfectly 'preserved' tenement (in all its bleakness); a gallery; and offers informative neighborhood walking tours often led by guides in period costume.

Orchard Street sign

*Lower East Side
Tenement Museum*

Orchard Street Sunday Market

Route 3

TriBeCa – ★ SoHo – ★★ Greenwich Village – East Vil-
lage – Gramercy Park – Madison Square Park

It is best to allow two days for this route.

One of the most common criticisms of New Yorkers is that
they never have any time for anything. They don't walk
anywhere, they run. And they have no time to speak in
complete words, let alone complete sentences: thus

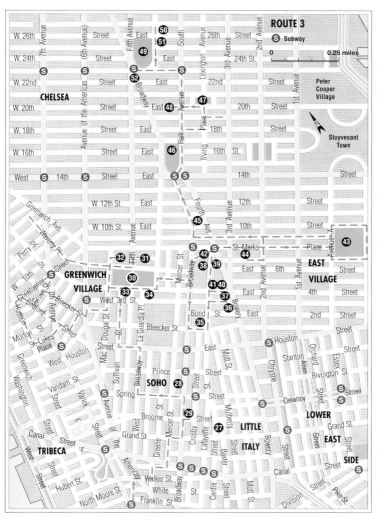

ROUTE 3

S Subway

0   0.25 miles

35

TriBeCa: warehouses have become galleries

SoHo: center for the avant-garde

Bloomingdale's becomes *Bloomie's,* Long Island becomes *the Island,* the area south of Houston Street is *SoHo,* and the triangular area below Canal Street is known familiarly as *TriBeCa.*

TriBeCa begins below Canal Street's western end and can be reached most easily via subway (get off at Franklin Street). In terms of geography, social make-up and origins, TriBeCa is an extension of **SoHo**. The galleries, interesting shops and off-beat restaurants which attract bankers and brokers from the Financial District for lunch are characteristic features of both districts. In the late 1960s, artists moved into the old houses and warehouses; it was they who saved the area south of Houston (pronounced HOWston rather than HEWston, by the way) from falling into decay. The warehouses stood empty back then, home to vagrants and bag ladies until gallery owners, painters and musicians suddenly realized that the spacious halls here were ideal for their purposes. Artists' studios could be set up with ease, there was more than enough room for sound and film studios too, and the rents were lower than in Chelsea and Greenwich Village, the classic New York arty areas. The first gallery was opened in SoHo in 1968, a second one followed a year later, and in 1971 four major gallery owners from uptown moved into the neighborhood. Restaurants followed, and real estate agents weren't far behind. Young artists who hadn't already made it had to move on. Then they discovered TriBeCa – and the whole procedure began again. TriBeCa is by no means as glitzy as SoHo, but it does possess two or three important avant-garde art centers, including the **Franklin Furnace** on Franklin Street, a combination museum-archive for bookworks by well-known downtown artists. The area also contains three of the best restaurants in the city: **Montrachet** (239 West Broadway), **Bouley** (165 Duane Street) and **Chanterelle** (2 Hudson Street).

SoHo's place as a mecca of the city's artistic culture was further enhanced in 1992 when a branch of the **Guggenheim Museum ㉘** was opened at 575 Broadway. It hosts temporary exhibitions of modern art. Also on Broadway are the **New Museum of Contemporary Art** (No 583) and the **Museum for African Art** (No 593).

There are many listed buildings in SoHo: between West Houston and Canal, West Broadway and Crosby Street lies the ★ **SoHo Cast Iron District**. Cast iron was a favored material during the 19th century for bridge and railway station construction, since large areas could be covered by placing prefabricated parts alongside one another. Cast iron was soon used for the construction of factories and warehouses, and the material had a priceless advantage: it was virtually fireproof, something much valued by New Yorkers due to the major conflagrations of 1835 and 1845.

Pretty as a picture

During the first half of the 19th century the area south of Houston Street was a busy business and residential quarter, particularly popular with New York's middle classes. There were theaters and places of entertainment; elegant hotels and large stores like Lord & Taylor or Tiffany's lined Broadway, which around 1850 gradually started to supplant the Bowery as the city's most important entertainment district.

37

After the Civil War (1861–5) the neighborhood's character changed. The shops moved northwards, many people left, and industry moved in instead. Because it was much quicker to construct buildings with cast iron than with, say, stone, factories, warehouses and workshops all sprang up virtually overnight. The aesthetic results of cast iron can be admired on the **Haughwout Building** ㉙, erected in 1857 on the corner of Broadway and Broome Street, and considered by many to be the finest example of American cast-iron architecture. The architect, John P Gaynor, gave it a Venetian-style exterior complete with Palladian arches; the building also contains the city's first-ever passenger elevator.

The cast-iron construction boom vanished as quickly as it came: the development of steel skeleton construction in around 1890 meant that skyscrapers could now be built, and cast iron became a thing of the past. In the previous 30 years, however, New York had set a world record for the largest number of buildings with cast-iron facades. In the 1970s, many of these structures would have disappeared for good were it not for those New Yorkers who successfully protested against plans to raze of much of the area to make way for a highway.

Those who don't only want to stroll around admiring buildings should definitely visit SoHo on a Saturday, when the galleries are open and artists and buyers pour into SoHo and TriBeCa to see and be seen. They all meet up in restau-

Galleries are open on Saturdays

rants and cafes, stroll about and dine out late. The area doesn't get busy until 10am or so, but activities continue very late into the night.

Another paradise for night-owls is ★★ **Greenwich Village**, easily reached from SoHo via Sullivan Street, which comes out into **Washington Square Park ③⓪**. On sunny days and balmy summer evenings it seems as if all the colorful life of the Village is concentrated here: folksingers strum guitars; students rollerskate and skateboard; esoteric street performers do their stuff. This little park was a center of the hippie movement in the late 1960s: the first ever 'smoke-in' took place here.

During its history, Washington Square has been used for almost every conceivable activity. Originally a potter's field, where the poor and unknown were buried, it later became a field of honor, a place of execution and a parade-ground. The first houses were built during the 1820s, and Washington Square soon became a desirable address. Several of these fine houses can still be seen along the north side of the square, where Fifth Avenue begins, and there is also an interesting view down **Washington Mews ③①**, a small cobbled street of row houses where the wealthy used to keep their horses stabled, and which are now highly sought-after residences.

A counterpart to the mews, accessible from Washington Square West Street, is **MacDougal Alley ③②**. Here too, former stables have been turned into attractive residential buildings. The 85ft (26m) high **memorial arch** dominating the square was originally planned as a temporary addition: the first version was made of wood, and stood here between 1889 and 1892 in commemoration of the centenary of the election of George Washington as the first president of the United States. After the celebration no-one wanted to part with it, so Stanford White was commissioned to build a white marble version of the arch.

The southern side of the square is dominated by the **Judson Memorial Baptist Church and Tower ③③**. Both the church and its tower were also designed by Stanford White in Italian Renaissance style, and completed in 1892 by White's firm of McKim, Mead and White. Today the tower is used by New York University (NYU), the main building of which is situated on the southeastern corner of Washington Square Park.

Further east, the **Loeb Student Center ③④** on the corner of La Guardia Place is also part of NYU. It was built in 1948 on the site of Marie Branchard's boarding house, an institution known as the 'house of genius' because of her illustrious guests, including writers Eugene O'Neill, Theodore Dreiser and Stephen Crane. The studio of painter John Sloan, a member of the group known as The Eight (*see page 52*), was situated a few houses further on.

A village of genius

In fact it's one big 'village of genius'. From the turn of the century onwards, Greenwich Village has been the home of the artistic avant-garde. The radical paper *Masses*, whose contributors included Maxim Gorki, Bertrand Russell and John Reed, had its offices here. In 1914, Gertrude Vanderbilt Whitney opened a gallery and provided a platform for contemporary artists, much of whose work was highly controversial. In 1916, members of the Playwrights' Theater settled on MacDougal Street and very soon achieved fame – Eugene O'Neill among them.

39

After World War II the Bohemian image of 'the Village' persisted. In the 1950s, the beatnik movement flowered (Jack Kerouac and Allen Ginsberg); in the 1960s and early '70s, hippies and anti-Vietnam war activists (Abbie Hoffman and Jerry Rubin). Christopher Street, on the other side of Sixth Avenue, became the center of the New York gay community. And suddenly the Village was chic – and expensive. The artists and activists moved out, the smart boutiques moved in. This is most evident on **Bleecker** and **MacDougal Streets**, with their rows of restaurants, cafés – some of which are very attractive – gift shops and souvenir stores.

Gay Pride on Christopher Street

Funky MacDougal Street

Beyond Sixth Avenue, the Village is less commercialized. A stroll through Waverly Place, Grove Street, Bedford Street or St Luke's Place – to name but a few of the loveliest byways – is a good introduction to the truly village-like character of this part of the city. It's almost like being in Europe: low houses, almost all of them 19th-century, rooftiles, pretty portals, leafy front gardens and plenty of trees. Unlike SoHo, where the streets are laid out more or less in grid-form, the streets in this part of the Village follow the same twisty routes they did back in the 18th century, when the bucolic village of Greenwich – as it was then known – was a popular summer refuge for colonial New Yorkers.

Shops for all tastes

Neo-Romanesque building at 376-383 Lafayette Street

Skidmore House: early 19th-century architecture

To discover East Village, go back to Washington Square. From here, Washington Place leads to a stretch of Broadway (just north of the museums mentioned on *page 36*) that's part of 'NoHo', a rather undefined area **no**rth of **Ho**uston.

Those keen on weird shops, colorful displays and student will find all he or she ever desired: crazy toyshops and souvenir shops, boutiques with fashion jewelry and expensive accessories. **Tower Records** is a huge music store at 692 Broadway and, a few blocks north at the corner of 12th Street, the **Strand bookstore** is one of the last survivors of what was once known as 'Booksellers' Row', offering 'eight miles' of used books.

Those interested in architecture and history should go via Bleecker Street to Lafayette Street: At No 65 Bleecker Street is the **Bayard-Condict Building** 🉟 (1897–9), the only work of Louis H Sullivan in New York. Sullivan worked predominantly in Chicago. He was a major exponent of the Chicago School, whose members became famous for the construction of the earliest skyscrapers; he also taught Frank Lloyd Wright. The six angels adorning the facade are not quite in keeping with the remainder – Sullivan was apparently forced to add them against his better judgment.

The former **Bond Street Savings Bank** 🉠 on the corner of Bond Street and the Bowery is worth a short detour south; it is a fine example of cast-iron architecture dating from 1874. Note too the former headquarters of the **New York Fire Department** 🉡 at 44 Great Jones Street, built in the Beaux Arts style in 1898; and also the imposing neo-Romanesque structure at **376–383 Lafayette Street** (corner of Great Jones Street); it was built in 1888 by architect Henry J Hardenbergh, famous for designing both the Plaza Hotel and the Dakota Building (*see pages 58 and 69*).

Great Jones Street formerly connected with **Lafayette Place**, the precursor of today's Lafayette Street, which looked very different indeed during the first half of the 19th century. It was a tree-lined cul-de-sac, and home to wealthy residents such as Jacob Astor and Cornelius Vanderbilt. They lived in **Colonnade Row** 🉢, which consisted of nine mansions and owes its name to their impressive colonnaded porticoes. Four of these buildings, which were erected in 1833, can still be admired today along the western side of Lafayette Street.

On the opposite side of the street is the **Joseph Papp Public Theater** 🉣, originally the Astor Library, and now named after the founder of the New York Shakespeare Festival. There are another two interesting early 19th-century buildings on 4th Street, which intersects with Lafayette: the **Old Merchant's House** 🉤, a museum at No 29; and the **Samuel Tredwell Skidmore House**, at No 37. At the

junction of 4th Street and Lafayette, the **DeVinne Press Building** was erected in 1885, and is a reminder of a time when the area around Lafayette Street was the center of the city's print trade.

The Old Merchant's House is a museum

Astor Place ⓸ angles east from Broadway to Third Avenue and contains two other things definitely worth seeing: the first – above ground – is the **kiosk** at the subway entrance, a copy of the cast-iron original, and the second is the restored subway station itself. The ceramic tiles on the walls display beavers – a clue to how the Astor family grew so wealthy. It all began when the 20-year-old John Jacob Astor emigrated from Germany to the USA in 1783. His career was a rags-to-riches story, though the rags in his case involved working in a fur shop. He worked his way up the ladder so quickly that he managed to open his own store within three years. Soon he was the most important fur dealer in the USA, and by the year 1800 had amassed a fortune of roughly $250,000, which he cleverly increased still further by investing in trade with Asia and in the New York property market. Branches of his firm sold furs across the entire continent. When he died in 1848 he was the richest man in America, and left behind a fortune of $20 million.

41

Cast-iron kiosk at Astor Place

From here walk down St Mark's Place, one of the city's liveliest thoroughfares, crammed with clubs, restaurants, boutiques and street peddlers. Geographically and historically, the **East Village** is part of the Lower East Side *(see page 33)*. The German names on some of the buildings are a reminder that this once used to be part of 'Little Germany' during the 19th century. It had its heyday at the beginning of the 1870s. **Tompkins Square** ⓸, further east, was the heart of the neighborhood. Avenue B, the commercial artery, was nicknamed 'German Broadway'. The basements contained workshops, the ground floors were shops, and goods were even sold outside on

'Strength in unity' – remnant of Little Germany

the sidewalks. There were beer halls, oyster saloons and grocery stores all along the avenue.

The area around Tompkins Square shared the fate of the Lower East Side. After the German community had moved away, other nationalities moved in: Russian Jews, Ukrainians and later, Puerto Ricans to name but a few. They all came to the New World seeking a better life, but found living conditions were squalid to say the least: whole families had to make do with one dark room without a lavatory. In the summer they suffered from the intense heat, and in winter they had to use coin-operated gas-heaters in order to keep warm.

The Lower East Side became increasingly impoverished as the 20th century progressed. In the decades that followed World War II no self-respecting person ventured further than First Avenue, which now formed a sort of demarcation line: the world of vice and the 'golden triangle' of the drug-dealers lay beyond it, in the ABC avenues and the streets around Tompkins Square. The fact that today you can poke around whimsical boutiques and eat soya bean salads and other hearty fare in local cafés is not just because the police stormed the center of the drug trade years ago. The area was most radically transformed by the young artists and musicians who found SoHo too expensive and moved here because rents were considerably cheaper than elsewhere.

Unfortunately the East Village is undergoing the same transformation as SoHo, TriBeCa and the West Village: artists followed by galleries followed by restaurants followed by property dealers. Already, rents around the recently restored Tompkins Square Park go at prices quite unaffordable for young artists.

The clubs and performance rooms that made the East Village so popular still exist, though things only really get

42

Street talk

A true survivor

going after 11pm. During the daytime the best policy is simply to stroll through the streets, pausing at places like **McSorley's Old Ale House**  back on the corner of 7th Street and Third Avenue, which dates from 1854 and successfully survived the decline of the area. A true drinking man's pub where women didn't break the sex barrier until 1970, it was one of Irish playwright Brendan Behan's favorite hangouts.

Between 8th and 9th Street on Broadway is where AT Stewart (*see page 30*) built his second department store in 1862; it took up an entire block and marked the start of Ladies' Mile, which extended as far as 23rd Street and owed its name to the fact that most of the customers patronizing the many department stores here were female. Carry on along Broadway, passing **Grace Church** , one of the city's loveliest ecclesiastical structures. Built in 1846, its exterior white marble, now a muted grey, was mined by convicts at infamous Sing Sing prison in upstate New York.

Grace Church

Continue as far as **Union Square** . A fashionable area in the mid-19th century, until recently this square had deteriorated and become a hangout for vagrants. However, with the advent of the greenmarket several years ago, along with a number of media-related businesses moving into the neighboring side streets, Union Square is becoming fashionable once again – a trend enhanced by restaurants like the Union Square Cafe (*see page 87*). Union Square exudes a particular charm on market days: on Mondays, Wednesdays, Fridays and Saturdays farmers arrive from the surrounding regions to sell their produce.

43

Fresh greens on Union Square

At the northeastern corner of Union Square, Park Avenue begins: follow it only briefly before turning right into 18th Street and then immediately left again into Irving Place. The block between Irving Place, Third Avenue, 18th Street and Gramercy Park South is known as 'Block Beautiful'. Its architects were strongly influenced by Paris and London. This is also true of **Gramercy Park** , situated between 20th and 21st Street. It was established in the 1830s by a wealthy lawyer named Samuel Ruggles along the lines of a London square; the pretty brick houses surrounding it – some with fancy iron balconies – were and still are inhabited by wealthy intellectuals and successful artists. Unfortunately for visitors, like many of its European counterparts the well-cared-for park itself is open only to local residents (who have keys to the wrought-iron gate).

Gramercy Park

Just around the corner on 20th Street, at No 28, is the house where US president **Theodore Roosevelt** was born (now a museum run by the National Park Service). Another landmark worth admiring is the national Arts Club (15 Gramercy Park South), built as a private home in 1884.

And since 1888, the magnificent building next to it has housed the **Players' Club**, a famous meeting-place for actors and theater people.

There's still a tradition of entertainment in this neighborhood, as evidenced a few streets further north by **Madison Square Park** ㊾, which lies between Fifth and Madison Avenues, from 23rd to 26th Street. Just to the north is the site of the original Madison Square Garden. Actually, there were two of them: the first was designed by the famous architect Stanford White in 1890; it was a proper palace, complete with theater, concert hall, roof-garden, restaurant, café and also a tower – the second highest in the city at that time. A second version was built further north, but was torn down in 1924, more than 20 years before Madison Square Garden moved to its present locale (*see page 48*).

Into the hands of justice

Today the first original site is home to the **New York Life Insurance Building** ㊿, the work of Cass Gilbert who also designed the Woolworth Building (*see page 28*). Designed in a mixture of styles, it was completed between 1926 and 1928. The lobby is particularly worth seeing. Along the park's eastern edge is a building that looks like a Greek temple but is actually the **Appellate Division of the New York State Supreme Court** (51), and was built between 1896 and 1900. The statues adorning the building indicate its function: Justice can be seen, as can Moses, Solomon, Justinian and Confucius.

Somewhat further south is a tower that looks best after dark. It is part of the complex of buildings belonging to the Metropolitan Life Insurance Company, and was modeled by architect Napoleon le Brun after the Campanile of St Mark's in Venice. Built in 1893 (and added to in 1909, 1932 and 1964), it's never been as eyecatching as its neighbor to the south, the **Flatiron Building** (52). Originally called the Fuller Building, this triangular skyscraper really does resemble an iron when observed from the corner of Fifth Avenue and Broadway.

The Flatiron Building

What really caused a stir when it was erected in 1902 though was not the building's appearance so much as its extraordinary height: 250ft (76m). People on the ground were convinced it would collapse if a storm came, but thanks to the new 'steel skeleton' construction methods of the day it is still standing today. The new building technique came from Chicago, as did the architect of the Flatiron, Daniel H Burnham. The construction of the Flatiron Building ushered in the skyscraper age, which radically changed the face of New York City over the next few decades.

Reflecting the area's growing reputation in media circles, the neighborhood is colloquially known as 'SoFi', which stands, of course, for 'South of Flatiron'.

Route 4

Empire State panorama

★★★ **The Empire State Building – Garment District – ★ Times Square – ★★ Rockefeller Center – ★★★ Museum of Modern Art**

This route through midtown Manhattan needs one or two days to complete. *See map, page 46.*

The route starts in a famous building on the corner of Fifth Avenue and 34th Street. The souvenir shop on the 86th floor sells giant plastic gorillas made in Taiwan: yes, it's King Kong, swatting at biplanes from the top of the ★★★ **Empire State Building** ⓼. The film *King Kong* was shot in 1933, and this was the obvious building to choose for its grand finale: the Empire State Building was just two years old and considered to be the eighth wonder of the world. At 1,250ft (381m) it was the tallest building on earth, and was only outdone by the World Trade Center in 1973. No less wondrous was the speed at which the Empire State was constructed: the whole procedure took just nine months. Its 6,500 windows need to be washed twice every month, and there are 73 elevators.

The lobby is superb: three stories high, faced with marble and decorated with bas-relief. There's more than enough time to admire it because the lines for the elevators tend to be very long indeed. The view from the top is worth the wait, however: the 86th floor has a glass-enclosed area and an outdoor promenade, while the observatory on the 102nd floor is completely enclosed (the viewing terraces are open till midnight; tickets are on sale until 11.25pm). Manhattan by night – or at dusk, when the lights start coming on – is particularly memorable.

The route now continues westwards along 34th Street as far as the **Garment District**. This area extends roughly

Going up

A stitch in time

from 30th Street to 40th Street, and from Sixth to Eighth Avenue. The garment trade, previously located on the Lower East Side (*see page 42*), shifted north at the beginning of the 20th century. In the traditional immigrant sweatshops, mostly dingy, windowless cellars, tailors and seamstresses slaved long hours for miserable wages. The move northwards brought an improvement in work conditions, less because of the new location than because the first trade unions had recently been formed, and were growing increasingly powerful. Work conditions in the

clothing industry were still an affront to human dignity, however, and it was only after 146 people had lost their lives in a Greenwich Village fire at the Triangle Shirtwaist Company in 1911 that strikes and mass protests finally brought about an improvement.

The Garment District still produces a great deal of the wearing apparel for women and children in America. On weekdays, the atmosphere in the streets around Seventh Avenue – the main commercial artery through the Garment District, and known locally as 'Fashion Avenue' –

Moving carpets

General Post Office

Macy's

is hectic and businesslike. Trucks block the streets, and pushcarts and clothing rails laden with skirts, coats and blouses clutter the sidewalks.

In the southern part of the Garment District, **Pennsylvania Station** is as ugly and uninviting as most modern railway stations. New Yorkers are now regretting the 1968 demolition of the original, architecturally imposing Penn Station. On the flat roof of the new station is **Madison Square Garden** (1968), world-famous as a sports arena and concert stadium (*see also page 44*). The **General Post Office** ⑤, situated opposite Penn Station between Eighth and Ninth Avenue is a neoclassical building erected by McKim, Mead and White at the beginning of the 20th century.

The area further west becomes less and less inviting, with few attractions save for the intrepid **Sea-Air-Space Museum**, a converted World War II aircraft carrier moored at Pier 86, of west 46th Street. Fans of modern architecture should, however, go and look at the **Jacob K Javits Convention Center** ⑤⑥, situated between West Side Highway and Eleventh Avenue north of 34th Street. This glass palace opened in 1986, and was designed and built by IM Pei & Partners. The 165ft (50m) high Crystal Palace Lobby is particularly impressive.

From here it's back to the junction of Broadway and Sixth Avenue, and into the world of consumption. Here, on Herald Square, stands **Macy's** ⑤⑦, said to be the biggest department store in the world. In recent years it has been competing increasingly often with the more upscale Bloomingdale's (*see page 59*). It's worth a visit just for the window displays; a stroll across the ground floor to take in the huge selection of goods and their tasteful presentation is also a very rewarding experience.

Macy's was built on the site of a former opera house where a major scandal occurred during the mid-19th century: Mrs William H Vanderbilt, a member of the city's monied aristocracy (her husband's fortune was an estimated $94 million), was denied the use of a paid box at the opera, since the opera house was firmly in the hands of old-established New Yorkers who wanted to have nothing to do with *parvenus* like the Astors and Vanderbilts. Her indignation did not last long, however: 65 millionaires joined forces, collected $1.5 million and built their own opera house, with 122 boxes – more than enough for all the Astors, Morgans, Rockefellers and Vanderbilts. It stood on the corner of Broadway and 40th Street, was opened in 1883, and was named the Metropolitan Opera House. The celebrated building finally closed its doors in 1966 after a nostalgic farewell gala; the Metropolitan Opera was re-opened that same year at the Lincoln Center (*see page 59*).

From Herald Square, follow Broadway northwards as far as 40th Street and **Broadway** 'proper', the street famous throughout the world. The name Broadway today is synonymous with theaters, shows, musicals, entertainment, and the glitzy world of the Great White Way, as this section of Broadway between 40th and 53rd streets was referred to after electric light made its appearance for the first time. Its heyday was in the 1920s and 30s, when there were over 80 theaters on and around Broadway. The most famous section was 42nd Street – so famous in fact that theater owners whose properties were actually on 41st or 43rd Street had passageways constructed through entire blocks of buildings just to be able to boast a 'Forty Second Street' address.

But in the late 1920s the cinema learned to talk and Broadway theater began to decline. The Great Depression added to Broadway's woes, turning many of the theaters along 42nd Street into burlesque houses and then cinema palaces. As it fell into decay the street developed a very different kind of fame – as a red-light district, becoming synonymous with drugs and prostitution.

Times Square

Nearby ★ **Times Square** 🄝 suffered a similar fate. Named after the famous *New York Times* newspaper, which moved into offices here in 1904, this long square at the junction of Broadway and Seventh Avenue is the traditional center of the busy Theater District; it is also the site of the city's boisterous annual New Year's Eve celebration. In the immediate vicinity, more than 35 Broadway theaters attract audiences to more than 30 new theatrical productions a year (in addition to such long-running London imports as *Cats* and *Miss Saigon*). And while many of the area's fine buildings were torn down to make way for faceless office blocks in the 1980s, things began to look up in the 1990s, when extensive rebuilding work, including hotels, restaurants and shops, began to take place. It is hoped that Times Square will once again be returned to its former glory.

While the area is in flux, however, aspects of its seedy past remain, so walk with a purpose, take care in the subway and keep your eye on any valuables. If you feel like enjoying a bird's-eye view, step into one of the 12 glass elevators at the **Marriott Marquis Hotel** 🄝 which go up to a revolving restaurant.

The route now continues onwards to 47th Street, to the brief section beyond Sixth Avenue, known as ★ **Diamond Row**. Eighty percent of the US diamond trade is transacted along the 270yds (250m) of street here – either inside the shops with their glittering displays, or simply out on the street: a few of the sellers carry their wares in their pockets in a piece of tissue paper that is traditionally folded. There are no contracts; deals are completed

Diamond Row has 80 percent of the US diamond trade

with a handshake. The Diamond Dealers Club supervises everything to ensure that no one breaks the strict code of honor. Anyone accused of double-dealing can expect to be banned from the international diamond trade altogether.

After a stroll along 47th Street, turn left into **Fifth Avenue**, one of the city's most famous shopping streets (*see page 58*).

St Patrick's Cathedral

Shortly before ★ **St Patrick's Cathedral** – a neo-Gothic structure built between 1858 and 1874 on the corner of Fifth Avenue and 50th Street – a small pedestrian mall, known as the **Promenade**, appears on the left-hand side between 49th and 50th Street, and leads to ★★ **Rockefeller Center**. This huge compound of office towers is a 'city within the city', and extends from Fifth to beyond Sixth Avenue and from 48th to north of 51st Street. It was designed to integrate several functions within a single complex: accommodation, work, shops, restaurants and entertainment. The basic architectural concept behind the scheme can be formulated as follows: an attempt to create space in all its different dimensions. Depth: the complex is served by an underground network of walkways. Height: the buildings grow narrower the higher they get, so that light can penetrate, and the high and low buildings were designed to avoid conveying any sense of being 'cooped up'. There is an abundance of space on the horizontal plane too: squares, open areas, broad streets and narrow passageways.

The centerpiece of the complex is the **Sunken Plaza** **60**, which serves as a skating rink in winter and an outdoor cafe in summer. Colorful flags flap quietly, and a golden *Prometheus* hovers in front of the waterfall. This piece of work by Paul Manship is the most well-known

50

Statue of Prometheus

but not the only artwork here in Rockefeller Center: there are over 100 paintings and sculptures here by more than 30 artists. Outside the **International Building** on Fifth Avenue, for instance, is Lee Lawrie's *Atlas*; another work by the same artist, *Wisdom*, can be seen above the entrance portal of the General Electric (formerly RCA) Building. Architecturally, this is the most important building in the complex, with its restrained art deco elegance.

International Building

The entire compound was financed by just one man: John D Rockefeller Jr. The Rockefeller name is of course synonymous with money, but the surprising thing about the Center is that John D managed to come up with the $125 million needed for its construction at a time when America was going through the worst depression in its history. The first 14 buildings were constructed between 1931 and 1940. Thousands of people who would otherwise have remained unemployed found work here.

Rockerfeller Center, Lower Plaza

The whole complex is extremely harmonious and self-contained, and this becomes very clear when one crosses over to Sixth Avenue and takes a look at what architects added to it during the 1960s: three similarly-shaped blocks, ugly, faceless, and gloomy-looking. The small plazas at their base are just as uninviting – such a contrast to the rest of Rockefeller Center.

The entrance to one of the highlights of the Rockefeller Center, the art deco ★ **Radio City Music Hall** ❻, is right here on Sixth Avenue. This theater, too, was built during the Great Depression – it was opened in 1932 – which makes the sheer amount of pomp, luxury and splendor inside all the more surprising. The six-story foyer contains a magnificent staircase, the seats are all upholstered in soft velvet, and the stage is as wide as a city block. The gold satin curtain weighs 3 tons and is raised and lowered by 13 motors. The sun, the moon and the stars appear at the touch of a button; likewise lightning and storm effects.

Radio City Music Hall

The enormous 6,200-seat auditorium was always sold out, even during the worst years of the Great Depression when the theater either presented the famous Rockettes revue group, or the very latest movies on the huge screen. It was only much later, with the arrival of television, that the owners began to have difficulty in filling the house. Rumors of demolition were rife, but then local New Yorkers amassed a small fortune to save their last great entertainment center, and Radio City Music Hall underwent restoration. Today it is a listed building, and hosts extravagant shows on a year-round basis. A guided tour is more than worthwhile (for times, tel: (212) 247 4777 or (212) 632 4041).

The ★★★ **Museum of Modern Art** ❻ (11 W 53rd Street) is well worth a visit, even for those who think they don't like modern art. Just as the Whitney Museum

MoMA – mecca for modern art

was the brainchild of Gertrude Vanderbilt Whitney (*see page 67*), so New York's MoMA was founded by one of the city's first ladies. Abby Rockefeller, the wife of John D Rockefeller Jr, was a passionate collector of modern art – much to her husband's distress. Her collection included works by such artists as Georgia O'Keefe, Pablo Picasso and Georges Braque, as well as painters from the group known as The Eight, who were exponents of the so-called Ashcan School. It is probably safe to assume that John D Jr had simply had enough of seeing these works dangling around his home when he decided to sacrifice a few million to his wife's passion and fulfill her dream of founding her very own museum.

It was opened in 1929, and ten years later the collection was shifted to its present home on 53rd Street. The building has undergone quite a few alterations since that time. In 1951, the famous architect Philip Johnson added two wings; during the 1960s several neighboring buildings were acquired; and in 1983 the western part of the building was extended and provided with a 42-story apartment tower. The latter was highly controversial: architecture critic Ada L Huxtable spoke of a 'marriage of culture and commerce' – for in order to finance its extension work the museum had sold its air rights (*see page 55*) to a private corporation. This made it possible to construct a much higher tower than local regulations permitted and led, in Huxtable's view, to the destruction of '53rd Street's special New York character'. With its 'little old buildings, brownstones and municipal structures', 53rd Street had been 'one of the most attractive and cosmopolitan side-streets in all Manhattan.' This unlikely marriage has obvious advantages too, though: the museum's exhibition space has now doubled, finally providing room for Cubists, Expressionists, Pop Artists, Dadaists, etc. About 30 percent of the permanent collection can now be placed on view.

MoMA is considered by many to be the most important museum of modern art in the world – modern art here defined as starting with the Impressionists in the 1880s: Van Gogh, Monet, Chagall, Matisse, Toulouse-Lautrec, De Chirico, Picasso, Miró, Pollock and Warhol are just a few of the artists represented. There is also an architecture and design section, with works by Tiffany, Thonet, Marcel Breuer and many others. Photography also has its own section, and MoMA is famous for its films. Foreign films, classics, works by young unknowns, plus all kinds of lectures and seminars – there's always something going on. In the midst of it all, an oasis of calm is provided by the Abby Aldrich Rockefeller Sculpture Garden, designed by Philip Johnson. Trees, benches, ponds, terraces, even summer evening concerts, are enhanced by the works of Miró, Picasso, Rodin, Moore.

Matisse at MoMA

Relax in the Sculpture Garden

Route 5

★ United Nations Headquarters – ★★ Grand Central
Station – Park Avenue – ★★ Fifth Avenue – Upper
East Side – Harlem

One day is enough for a stroll from United Nations Head-
quarters (including a tour inside) as far as the Roosevelt
Island Tramway. More time should be allowed for the
Upper East Side and Harlem. *See map, page 45/6.*

The feeling one gets that each neighborhood in New York
has its own special set of rules, often incomprehensible
to outsiders, is nowhere more clear than in the small area
bounded by the East River, First Avenue, 42nd and 48th
Street: not even the laws of the USA are valid here! Don't
worry, though: this route starts in a very respectable area,
far from any crime or squalor. The fact that the area occupied by ★ **United Nations Headquarters** has its own
rules is a sign of exclusivity. The representatives from over
150 countries who work here enjoy a special kind of diplo-
matic immunity – often a source of irritation to the people of Manhattan because it means that UN employees can
park their cars wherever they like.

*United Nations Headquarters
and sculpture*

53

United Nations Headquarters consists of four buildings
behind a long row of colorful flags – one for each member country. There are artistic contributions from each
country here too: the buildings and gardens contain many
different sculptures, tapestries and paintings.

Before the UN arrived, the site was occupied by slaugh-
terhouses, glue factories, breweries and light industry. Not
only the smell and the noise but also the sight of the area
must have been very unpleasant: the architects who designed and built the apartment complex known as **Tudor City** ⓰ on 42nd Street avoided putting any windows
in its east facade, despite a good view of the river.

Tudor City

The turnaround came at the end of World War II. The
United Nations Organization was founded in San Fran-
cisco in 1945, as the successor to the League of Nations.
The problem of financing and finding it a suitable headquarters was solved by New York's John D Rockefeller
Jr; he purchased an $8.5 million-site overlooking the East
River and made a present of it to the UNO, while the USA
issued an interest-free credit of $67 million. The **Secre-
tariat Building** ⓰, with its narrow tower, was completed
in 1950. It was followed by the **Conference Building** ⓰,
the lowest building in the complex, the **General Assembly Building** ⓰, which serves as an auditorium, and finally by the **Dag Hammarskjöld Library** ⓰.

The team of architects who worked on the buildings
was also multinational: Le Corbusier (France), Oscar

Ford Foundation atrium

A famous landmark: the Chrysler Building and lobby

Niemeyer (Brazil), and Sven Markelius (Sweden), among others. The complex as a whole is by no means an architectural masterpiece – Le Corbusier distanced himself from it in later life. Nevertheless, this center of international decision-making is still worth a visit (tickets from the lobby of the General Assembly Building; *see page 81*). In addition, the UN's giftshop contains some very fine crafts and souvenirs from all over the world.

From the main exit, walk a few steps southwards before turning left, i.e. west, on 42nd Street. The eastern end of the street is very different from its sin-city section around Times Square (*see page 49*). Tudor City, for instance, is a very desirable address, and the whole area here is a paradise for lovers of art deco. First, though, how about a quick dose of tranquillity: the 130ft (40m) high atrium of the **Ford Foundation Building** (321 E 42nd Street). This is no ordinary atrium, but a third of an acre of mature trees and shrubs. There's even a brook. Passers-by are welcome to step inside and relax.

Directly opposite the Ford Foundation Building, between Second and Third Avenue, is the ***Daily News* Building** ❻❾ (220 E 42nd Street). Built in 1930, it has a magnificent entrance hall with a huge revolving globe. The newspaper was due to move to new digs in 1995, but it is hoped any new tenants will retain the name and character of the high-rise immortalized in the film *Superman* as headquarters for the fictional *Daily Planet*.

Another art deco jewel can be found on the corner of 42nd Street and Lexington Avenue: the ★★ **Chrysler Building** ❼⓿. Its unconventional tower, with stainless steel arches glinting in the sun and illuminated at night, is perhaps the most aesthetically satisfying in the New York skyline. The lobby is also fascinating, with its grained marble and chrome decor, enhanced by epic murals depicting transportation and human endeavour. Commissioned by automobile maker Walter P Chrysler, this 1,048ft (320m) high building was the tallest in New York on its completion in 1930, but was soon surpassed by the Empire State.

On the other side of Lexington Avenue is a more modern example of egomania: property mogul Donald Trump's **Grand Hyatt Hotel** ❼❶, formerly the Commodore Hotel and rebuilt in 1980 by architects Gruzen & Partner and Der Scott. The lobby is typical of Trump's bombastic style. Reflected in the glass facade of the hotel are two other buildings with fine lobbys of their own: the **Chanin Building** ❼❷ and the **Bowery Savings Bank** ❼❸, both of them dating from the 1920s.

The **Whitney Museum of American Art at Philip Morris** ❼❹, on the corner of 42nd Street and Park Avenue, holds alternating exhibitions of contemporary art (admission to the gallery and sculpture court is free).

Now a short detour, to the **New York Public Library** ⑦. This Beaux Arts building dates from 1911. Designed by architects Carrère & Hastings, it contains 9 million books. Alternating exhibitions on varying themes are held in Gottesman Hall. The steps outside the library are a popular oasis for resting shoppers, students and tourists; Bryant Park, which stretches behind the library to Sixth Avenue, is another pleasant spot, restored and planted with shrubs and flowers, and the site of various special events.

Generally speaking, East 42nd Street is not the place to find good restaurants. Amazingly enough, though, the best place to eat round here is inside ★★ **Grand Central Station** ⑦, but that shouldn't deter gourmets unduly. Despite its pub-like atmosphere, the **Oyster Bar** between the station's main and lower levels is considered by many to be the best seafood restaurant in the city.

The station was completed in 1913 and is a fine example of the Beaux Arts style. The main concourse with its pale blue ceiling depicting the celestial constellations is 115ft (35m) high, 125ft (38m) wide, and more than twice as long. Grand Central Terminal has been a listed building since the 1970s.

Towering above the railway station is the **MetLife** (formerly PanAm) **Building** ⑦, built in 1963 by Walter Gropius. It is an early example of something which has become a bit of a hobby with the city's property dealers: the buying and selling of 'air rights'. This takes place as follows: the owner of a low-rise building promises not to use up the construction height available to him and sells the air rights to his neighbor. The latter is then allowed either to build over the lower building, or add the same number of feet to his building that were lacking in the lower one. It all turns out to be highly lucrative for the owners of smaller buildings, despite contributing little to the aesthetics of the city skyline.

Grand Central's Oyster Bar
New York's Public Library

MetLife towers above the station

The Waldorf-Astoria remains a top-class establishment

It's possible to walk straight through the station and the lobby of the MetLife Building to reach **Park Avenue**, one of New York's most exclusive thoroughfares. Some of the shops here only open their doors to customers by appointment, and those who live here can be said to have 'made it'. The avenue also boasts the famous **Waldorf-Astoria Hotel** ⓲. Though less exclusive now than several other hotels in the city, alongside the Plaza it remains the most famous hotel in New York. The reception for the Apollo 11 astronauts (after the first-ever moon landing) took place here; kings, queens, heads of state and the world's wealthiest stay here, as do famous politicians and artists. One side-effect of all this fame is that the lobby is usually packed with tourists admiring the art deco work and soaking up the Waldorf atmosphere – often a source of irritation for paying guests.

On the corner of Lexington Avenue and 51st Street, the **General Electric Building** was built in 1931. The facade has several neo-Gothic features and the art deco lobby is worth a visit.

The stroll back to Park Avenue via 52nd Street also passes two buildings of historic importance. The **Seagram Building** ⓳ was designed by Mies van der Rohe in 1958, who caused a stir by being the first architect in Manhattan not to use all the construction space he had available: he left a plaza out in front. Others soon followed his example, and several other plazas for public use appeared. **Lever House** ⓴ between 53rd and 54th Street, was also a trendsetter: built in 1952 it was the city's first-ever glass-curtained skyscraper.

Walk eastwards along 53rd Street as far as Lexington Avenue and the **Citicorp Center** ㉑, built in 1978. Apart from its aesthetic appeal – with its distinctive sloping roofline, it's considered the most attractive post-modern structure in New York – it also contains numerous restau-

The Seagram Building

rants and shopping arcades, located within an interior
'landscape' of flowerbeds, trees and fountains. The Citicorp Center is 915ft (279m) high, and rests on 130ft (40m)
high pillars. Air rights had to be bought here, too. St Peter's Church owned them, surrendering them on condition
that the church be incorporated into the new building.

The route now continues westwards via 54th Street, and
then bears right onto Madison Avenue. Two controversial
examples of post-modern architecture stand side-by-side
between 55th and 57th Street. The **AT&T Building** ㉜,
designed by Philip Johnson, completed in 1983, and now
leased by Sony, has been both heralded and criticized as
a post-modernist leap back to earlier styles. The building is inhospitable, though, and the general opinion seems
to be 'nice material – shame about the design'. Next door
to it, the **IBM Building** ㉝, built in 1984, contains a 'gift
to the community' in the form of a spacious ground-level
atrium dotted with tables, chairs and slender bamboo trees.
The atrium is a good place to relax with a cup of coffee
before entering the glitzy world of Donald Trump – either
via the IBM lobby, which is the equivalent of the 'back
door', or better still via Fifth Avenue. The atrium of the
building known as **Trump Tower** ㉞ has to be seen to
be believed. With its brass, polished marble and waterfall,
it reflects the multi-millionaire's sense of showmanship.
The shops here are pricey, to say the least; the rents for
them and the luxury apartments overhead astronomical.

Trump Tower shop

Even though Trump's star now seems to be on the wane,
his success story is in many ways typical of New York.
It began in the 1970s, when the city was threatened with
bankruptcy and the large firms all seemed to be leaving.
It was during this period that Trump bought real estate
at knockdown prices – later on, of course, property prices
rocketed. The city has Trump and similar speculators to at
least partially thank for its new lease of life during the
1980s, but he and others like him were also largely responsible for increasing the gap between rich and poor.
Formerly, millionaires often counterbalanced their wealth
with philanthropy, and supported the city's social and cultural life. Trump's philosophy is clear, however: New York
has become a city for the super-rich, with no room left
for the poor. This is pure cynicism when one considers the
city's 100,000 homeless, and the fact that almost 2 million
of its population live below the poverty line.

Diamond's are forever

Next door to Trump Tower is the famous **Tiffany's**,
where jewelry, pearl-studded combs, diadems and all that
glitters can be bought for a great deal of money indeed.
Despite its high-carat name, Tiffany's was on the verge
of bankruptcy at the end of the 1970s and was purchased
by the Avon cosmetics firm. But the combination turned
out to be bad for business – those happy to fork out for

Tiffany's wares were unhappy to be reminded of cheap Avon products (the store happily regained its independence in 1984). Meanwhile, Donald Trump, who had just purchased a bankrupt department store next door, exploited this situation and offered $5 million for Tiffany's air rights. This allowed him to build 68 stories high in the most expensive part of Manhattan.

The section of ★★ **Fifth Avenue** near Central Park really is a very desirable address; further south, more and more cheap electrical goods stores and import-export shops have sprung up, while large department stores such as B Altman go bust. There again, this famous store caused quite a scandal when it first opened on the corner of 34th Street in 1906: the neighbors were against the idea of a commercial building in their select residential area. In the 1880s, the corner of Fifth Avenue and 34th Street had been a mecca for high society in the city. The elegant brownstone mansion of top society lady Mrs Caroline Astor stood here, for instance. It contained a ballroom large enough to accommodate 400 guests, and those not accepted into 'The Four Hundred', as it was called, could say goodbye to social life altogether. Family feuds finally forced Mrs Astor to move to the northern part of Fifth Avenue. The area was a wilderness, but no sooner had she moved there than all the city's wealthy followed. Magnificent mansions sprang up and the southern part of Fifth Avenue became what it has always been since then: a shopping street.

The most exclusive shops can be found between 48th and 59th Street, between Brentano's bookstore and the celebrated FAO Schwarz toyshop. Many of the luxury stores have their own liveried doormen, and distinguished-looking ladies can often be observed alighting from long black limousines. All the big names are here: Gucci, Valentino, Cartier, Bergdorf-Goodman, Van Cleef & Arpels, Harry Winston, Tiffany. Yet to look at it, Fifth Avenue often seems less than exclusive. The contrast between rich and poor in New York is no more glaring than it is here: street vendors selling cheap watches stand outside the most expensive boutiques, and homeless men beg for a few cents while hundred-dollar notes change hands nearby.

Providing a glorious finale to this stretch of Fifth Avenue is the famous ★ **Plaza Hotel** ㉟ overlooking Central Park. This architectural jewel, built in 1904 in the style of a French chateau, was bought by Donald Trump in 1988 for $410 million. Emperors, film stars and presidents have all stayed at this legendary hotel. Despite its astronomical room prices, The Plaza is definitely worth a visit. A drink in the famous Oak Bar, or a meal in the Palm Court are a lot less of a strain on the wallet than booking a suite.

In front of the hotel, the Pulitzer Fountain commemorates the famous journalist and publisher, while horse-

Brentano's for books

Fifth Avenue transportation

Statue at Grand Army Plaza

drawn carriages stand on the corner of Central Park and **Grand Army Plaza**, waiting to whisk their passengers away from the noise and bustle (for a description of Central Park *see page 63*).

Your carriage awaits

The route now heads east along 59th Street, back to Lexington Avenue. Along the way, one of the most recent products of the 1980s construction boom can be admired: a high-rise made of blue glass, the top of which resembles a thick pencil. Designed by Chicago architect Helmut Jahn, this building ⑧⑥ (750 Lexington Avenue) is particularly interesting when observed from 57th Street. On the corner of Lexington Avenue and 57th Street is another modern structure, designed by William Pedersen, which has received acclaim for the originality of its 'corner solution'.

Helmut Jahn building

Back into the world of consumerism: the famous department store of **Bloomingdale's** ⑧⑦ takes up the entire block between Lexington and Third Avenue, 59th and 60th Street. 'Bloomie's' is part of New York mythology, a perfectly organized, seven-story consumer paradise. Whatever you're looking for, this store has it all. On the corner of Second Avenue and 60th Street is the **Roosevelt Island Tramway** ⑧⑧, a cable car that travels across the East River to Roosevelt Island, an oasis of tranquillity containing one main street, a church, and a few restaurants.

59

59th Street marks the border between two worlds: midtown and the **Upper East Side**, where the city's hectic pace suddenly gives way to shady side streets and elegant houses. The shopping along Madison Avenue, starting with **Barney's** at 60th Street and continuing north in a splendid aggregation of stylish boutiques, is justly famous. The Upper East Side extends northwards as far as 96th Street. The traditionally Latino East Harlem begins north of 96th Street and leads into **Harlem** itself.

Named Nieuw Haarlem by the Dutch, Harlem became post-colonial New York City's first suburb: Alexander Hamilton, the country's first Secretary of the Treasury, had a home here, which today is a national park site. The railroad, and later the subway, led to an influx of European immigrants, but by 1910 or so, when African-Americans began moving into homes on 134th Street, white residents began to move out and Harlem soon became a primarily black neighborhood. Unfortunately, as in certain other areas in the city, it's not necessarily a good idea for first-time tourists to wander around on their own; better to join with a tour that stops at such landmarks as the **Studio Museum** (West 125th Street); the **Schomburg Center for Research in Black Culture** (Lenox Avenue and 135th Street); the famous **Apollo Theater**; and the beautifully preserved townhouses along 138th and 139th Streets, between Seventh and Eighth Avenues, that were designed by Stanford White and are commonly known as '**Striver's Row**'.

Streetwise shopping in Harlem

The Cloisters

UPPER WEST SIDE

West 96th Street
West 94th
W. 92nd Street
W. 90th Street
West 88th Street
West 86th Street
West 84th Street
W. 82nd Street
W. 80th Street
West 78th Street
West 76th Street
West 74th Street
West 72nd Street
West 70th Street
Lincoln Towers
W. 68th Street
66th Street
64th St.
60th Street

Broadway
Amsterdam Avenue
Columbus Avenue
West End Avenue
Central Park West
Riverside Drive
Hudson Parkway
Henry Hudson Parkway

CENTRAL PARK

Transverse Rd. No. 4

Receiving Reservoir

Transverse Rd. No. 3

The Great Lawn

Belvedere Lake

Transverse Rd. No. 2

CENTRAL PARK

The Lake

West Drive
East Drive

The Sheep Meadow

Transverse Rd. No 1

Heckscher Playground

The Pond

Central Park South

Miller Highway

108
109
107
106
105
104
103
102
101
100
99
98
94
93
92
91
89
7
6

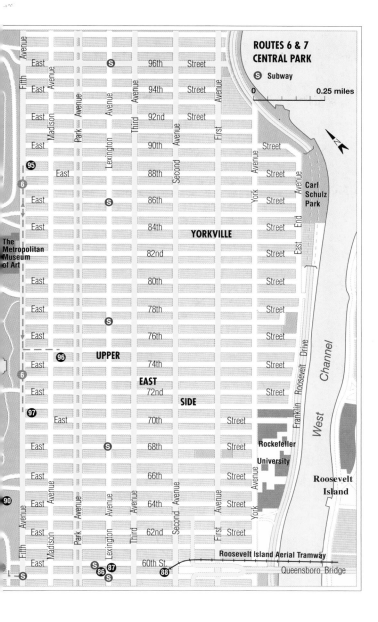

**ROUTES 6 & 7
CENTRAL PARK**

Ⓢ Subway

0   0.25 miles

61

Summer in the city

Route 6

★★ **Central Park** – ★★★ **Metropolitan Museum of Art** – ★★ **Solomon R Guggenheim Museum** – ★ **Whitney Museum of American Art** – ★ **Frick Collection**.

A substantial Sunday brunch is the best preparation for a pleasant stroll through Central Park. Even if you stop every few yards to marvel at the weekend antics of New Yorkers, it won't take more than half a day to cover the route to the Metropolitan Museum of Art described here.

If the plans of those who designed Manhattan had been followed to the letter, today it would be nothing more than a concrete jungle. There wouldn't have been anywhere to jog, picnic, ice-skate or sunbathe; in short, there wouldn't have been any ★★ **Central Park**. The members of the commission that decided Manhattan's architectural future in 1811 had only allowed enough room for four tiny squares of green; they wanted the rest of the island developed. If fate had placed New York on a small river like the Thames or the Seine, they claimed, open spaces would certainly have had to be created to guarantee enough fresh air. However, since Manhattan was next to the sea, the situation was different. Also, land prices were so high that economic considerations had to be given priority.

Bladerunners

New Yorkers soon experienced the consequences of this way of thinking. Between 1820 and 1840 the city's population swelled from 124,000 to 313,000, and Manhattan island's riverside spaces were suddenly covered with warehouses, dockyards and other installations. Voices were soon raised in protest. William Cullen Bryant, the publisher of the *New York Evening Post* and also a poet, the internationally famous author Washington Irving, painters, landscape architects and many others all insisted that an area of land at the center of the island be kept free of development and turned into parkland. In 1856 the decision was finally made: the city purchased a 2½ mile (4km) long, narrow strip of land between Eighth and Fifth Avenue, 59th and 110th Street. The hefty $5.5 million price for the 840 acre (240ha) area was attributed to the fact that the local property speculators had had more than enough time to prepare for the deal.

Strolling along the paths today, listening to the birds and admiring the lakes, meadows and trees, it's hard to imagine that the park is man-made and that in the mid-19th century this whole area was nothing but an evil-smelling swamp full of thin brushwood, boulders and stones. The only proper buildings here were a blockhouse and the city arsenal; the other 'structures' – as far as they could be termed such – provided temporary and miserable accommodation for goat-herders and squatters. They were quickly driven out when the developers turned up. The swamps were drained, bridges and roads were built, and wagonloads of earth were brought in so that thousands of trees and plants could grow. The workmen followed the plans of Frederick Law Olmsted and Calvert Vaux, the two architects who had won the Central Park design competition in 1857 and were now making their dream a reality.

Central Park sports

Landscape architects must possess certain visionary qualities, for how else can they predict how their work will evolve? It's doubtful, though, whether Olmsted and Vaux had the slightest idea of the range of activity that goes on in Central Park today: youths, stripped to the waist, dancing deliriously on roller-skates, film stars jogging along almost hidden by their bodyguards, tens of thousands of people covering the meadows for open-air concerts, and now and then the odd mugging or murder making the headlines.

Which brings us to the theme of safety in Central Park. Generally speaking, crime on average is lower in the park than elsewhere in the city. However, there are a couple of basic rules that should be followed:

1 Leave the park before dusk. Never come here at night, unless for one of the summer evening concerts.
2 Stick to the routes where people are, and avoid quiet, secluded corners.
3 Bring a friend (or two); there's always more safety in numbers.

The best day of the week to appreciate Central Park is on Sundays, when most of Manhattan is deserted and there are 1.5 million fewer people in the city than on the hectic weekdays. The commuters stay in the suburbs, and

64

Bethesda Fountain

Belvedere Castle

the Manhattanites have the island to themselves. New York suddenly becomes calmer, cozier and more relaxed, and Fifth Avenue fills with pedestrians who, after a substantial brunch, are irresistibly drawn to the park to stroll, play, cycle, canoe, drink coffee, or just to see and be seen. Everyone seems to be part of the same big show: from well-to-do ladies from the Upper East Side walking their poodles to athletic teenagers showing off their skateboarding prowess.

The best route to take for a stroll is from the park entrance near Grand Army Plaza, 59th Street and the corner of Fifth Avenue, up to the Lake. This route passes the Pond, the western side of which is a bird sanctuary, and also the **Wollman Memorial Rink** ❽❾, which offers either rollerskating or iceskating depending on the time of year. The newly-renovated **Zoo** ❾⓿ is definitely worth visiting. Information about the park's other attractions can be obtained from the Visitor Centre at the **Dairy** ❾❶ ; this is the place to go for maps and directions to places like **Strawberry Fields**, Yoko Ono's memorial to John Lennon, as well as special exhibits on the park's history and the excellent daily tours led by Urban Park Rangers. Continue along the mall – a long avenue lined with trees and busts of famous artists (Beethoven, Burns, Shakespeare, Scott, etc) where there's always something going on – as far as **Bethesda Fountain** ❾❷ and the Lake. To the north of the Lake, at the highest point of Central Park, **Belvedere Castle** ❾❸ exudes medieval romanticism; next door is the open-air **Delacorte Theater** ❾❹, and not far away the **Great Lawn** is where music lovers spread their blankets for free summer evening concert performances.

It's only a few steps from here to the only large building allowed in the park: the ★★★ **Metropolitan Museum of Art** (on Fifth Avenue between 80th and 84th Street). Calvert Vaux had a hand in its design, though all that remains of the original brownstone structure of 1880 is a small section that can still be seen from the direction of the park. More sections and wings have been added continually to cope with the massive amount of art here, and the present-day building – although stretching between 80th and 84th Streets – still holds less than half the museum's permanent collection of over 3 million objects. The two most recent architectural additions are the three-story American Wing (1980) and the Lila Acheson Wallace Wing (1987); the latter includes a roof-garden with a superb view of Central Park. In addition, the museum recently announced plans for the enlargement of its Greek and Roman galleries as well as the creation of several new exhibit spaces, contained within the framework of the existing structure.

Metropolitan Museum of Art

There's no way round it, unfortunately: in order to avoid spending several weeks inside the Metropolitan Museum one does have to concentrate on just a few rooms. There is an information desk in the museum's 'Great Hall' (just inside the main entrance). Here is a short summary of what can be found inside:

65

Ground Floor: *Costume Institute* (clothing from 17th to 20th centuries; alternating exhibitions); *Robert Lehman Collection* (private collection taking up two floors; 3,000 works of art donated to the museum by Robert Lehman, most of them European including works by Rembrandt, Goya, Van Gogh and Matisse); *Uris Center for Education* (classrooms and auditorium).

Main Floor: *Egyptian Wing* (world-famous Egyptian art collection; highlight here is the Temple of Dendur); *Greek and Roman Art* (parts of the collection are among the museum's oldest exhibits; of particular interest is the bedroom of a villa from Boscoreale near Pompeii dating from AD79; *Medieval Art* (magnificently presented exhibits, 7th–16th century); *European Sculpture and Decorative Art* (various galleries containing reconstructions of rooms from European palaces and mansions); *Arms and Armor*; *Michael C Rockefeller Wing* (Precolumbian art, tribal art and cult artifacts from Africa and Oceania); *American Wing* (63 galleries distributed across the Main and Second Floors, containing every possible manifestation of American art, including paintings, sculpture, decorative art, period rooms, etc); *Lila Acheson Wallace Wing* (two floors and the magnificent roof-garden are devoted to 20th-century art; mostly American artists).

The Chess Players

One of the Met's Monets

Second Floor: *Nineteenth-Century European Paintings and Sculpture* (a recent 21-gallery addition); *European Paintings* (including a number of Rembrandts); *Islamic Art*; *South and Southeast Asian Art*; *Japanese Art*; *Chinese Art*; *Ancient Near Eastern Art* (oldest exhibits here date from 6000BC); *Drawings, Prints and Photographs* (artists represented include Leonardo da Vinci, Titian, Michelangelo, Turner and Degas); *Musical Instruments* (including three Stradivari). Plus: *Greek and Roman Art*, *20th Century Art* and *American Wing* exhibits, continued from the main floor.

This great treasure trove of art, along with a regular series of spectacular special exhibitions, has made the Metropolitan Museum of Art one of the world's most impressive centers of culture. And names such as the Robert Lehman Collection and the Lila Acheson Wallace Wing make it clear that, like many American cultural institutions, the Metropolitan has historically benefited from the largesse of wealthy patrons. Something which may also explain why such a large number of museums are found nearby: when Mrs Caroline Astor moved house to the Upper East Side (*see page 58*), the northern part of Fifth Avenue became the most desirable place to live in the whole of the city. Whoever could afford it built villas facing Central Park, and many of the buildings have now become foundations and institutes. **The Institute for Jewish Research**, for instance, is housed in a magnificent 1911 mansion that was once the home of Mrs Cornelius Vanderbilt; the **Cooper-Hewitt Museum of Design** is inside the former villa of millionaire Andrew Carnegie (Fifth Avenue/91st Street; *see page 58*); Solomon R Guggenheim had the architecturally bizarre Guggenheim Museum *(see below)* built on his land.

This so-called 'Museum Mile' actually extends more than a mile (from 82nd to 104th Street). Because of the sheer amount cultural institutions in the vicinity, a certain amount of selectiveness is required. The following three, however, shouldn't be missed:

Outside and inside the Guggenheim

The ★★ **Solomon R Guggenheim Museum** Ⓥ (Fifth Avenue/89th Street) is worth visiting just for its architecture: it was designed by Frank Lloyd Wright. From the outside it resembles an upturned snail-shell; inside, the spiral ramp affords continually new perspectives on the artworks displayed.

The museum was opened in 1959 somewhat later than planned – 16 years in fact – due to bureaucracy and protests from local residents. Guggenheim and Frank Lloyd Wright had both already died. When it was finally ready it was an architectural sensation, but still had far too little room for Guggenheim's mammoth collection – the copper magnate owned over 4,000 paintings, sculptures and drawings. A new building – which rather dominates the original – was opened in 1992 to provide more exhibition space. Highlights here include the largest collection of Kandinskys in the world, also works by Picasso, Chagall, Mondrian, Marc, Miró, Renoir, Manet and many others.

The ★ **Whitney Museum of American Art** ⓰ has a midtown branch, too (*see page 54*), but its main building is on the corner of Madison Avenue and 75th Street. The collection was the idea of Gertrude Vanderbilt Whitney, a sculptor who also happened to be rich, and who helped young artists to exhibit their work in Greenwich Village as early as the 1930s.

In contrast to the Museum of Modern Art, the Whitney Museum exclusively exhibits 20th-century American art. The latest paintings and sculptures are always presented each autumn. 'Classics' among the moderns include Lichtenstein, Pollock, Rauschenberg and Shan. One real highlight here must not be missed: the 2,000 or so works by Edward Hopper.

Little Big Painting by Lichtenstein

The ★ **Frick Collection** ⓱ (Fifth Avenue/70th Street), a collection of art treasures assembled by steel manufacturer Henry Clay Frick, is housed in his former palazzo, which was built in the French neoclassical style in 1913. Efforts have been made to keep the house more of a house and less of a museum; it's like being the guest of a man who can afford to surround himself with select works of art. The tiny roofed inner courtyard is particularly attractive. Goya, Titian, El Greco, Vermeer and Renoir are just a few of the artists represented here.

67

Portrait by Titian
The Frick's Garden Court

The Dakota

Route 7

Upper West Side and ★ The Cloisters

It's best to plan a full day for Route 7, not including a visit to The Cloisters in the north. *See map, page 60.*

West of Central Park, something strange happens to Manhattan: the avenues which had to content themselves with being plain numbers as far as 59th Street suddenly grow names again. Eighth becomes Central Park West, Ninth becomes Columbus Avenue, Tenth becomes Amsterdam Avenue and Eleventh becomes West End Avenue.

Why the name change? It's all to do with image. When the Upper West Side came into existence at the end of the 19th century, local property owners planned to create an elegant residential area for the wealthy. The negative image of Eighth, Ninth, Tenth and Eleventh Avenue stood in their way. These weren't 'good addresses', and didn't look good on visiting cards. So they were renamed, suddenly sounded more exclusive – and local property prices started to rise.

The first building to raise the tone of the area west of the park was the American Museum of Natural History, which was opened in 1877. Seven years after that, the first wealthy entrepreneur moved up to the west: Edward Clark. As heir to the Singer Sewing Machine Company fortune, Clark had more than enough money to build an apartment house resembling a castle next to the park, on a level with 72nd Street, and he even surrounded it with a moat. Clark created this elevated atmosphere on purpose, to set his future tenants at ease: New York's upper class of that time still found the idea of an apartment house extremely vulgar. As for the location of the 'castle': Fifth Avenue society turned up its nose at it. So far removed from city life, well, it was just as if one lived in the Dakota Territory out west, they joked – and suddenly the house had a nickname: the *Dakota*.

Despite all the reservations everyone may have had, the Upper West Side had its way. The construction of the 'Ninth Avenue El' (1878), one of New York's first and once prevalent raised railways, brought the Dakota closer to the rest of the city, and many apartment houses were built that provided accommodation for people who found downtown or the Lower East Side too cramped and who could still afford to escape. For them, moving to the Upper West Side symbolized the first rung on the ladder to social success. Even though some luxury apartment houses and addresses, like Central Park West or Riverside Drive, were reserved for the very wealthy, the atmosphere of the Upper West Side during the first phase of its settlement was solidly middle-class.

In later decades, the Upper West Side developed into a favorite address for intellectuals. Actors, musicians and writers who have lived and continue to live here include Hannah Arendt, Anaïs Nin, Yehudi Menuhin, John Lennon, Scott Fitzgerald, Isaac Bashevis Singer, Billy Joel, Mick Jagger, Harry Belafonte and Paul Simon, to name but a few.

Columbus Circle

A stroll round the Upper West Side begins on **Columbus Circle 98**, a hectic, traffic-filled square. At its center, Columbus stands on a column, and on its southern side is the **New York Convention & Visitors Bureau**, the tourist information center (*see page 98*).

Broadway is the shortest route from here to the ★ **Lincoln Center for the Performing Arts 99**, but a more scenic way to get to Lincoln Center is to stroll along Central Park and then turn down 63rd Street, which leads directly to it. This conglomeration is the heart of mainstream New York culture: the **Metropolitan Opera House**, the **New York State Theater**, which is shared by the **New York City Ballet** and the **New York City Opera**, **Avery Fisher Hall**, home of the New York Philharmonic, **Alice Tully Hall**, headquarters of the Lincoln Center Chamber Music Society, and the **Juilliard School**, where young hopefuls study and give concerts (often for free).

Flying the flag over the Lincoln Center

Twelve blocks had to be demolished to make way for this 'temple of the muses', and 1,500 people rehoused. Five architects were commissioned for the various buildings: Max Abramovitz, Philip Johnson, Wallace K Harrison, Eero Saarinen and Pietro Bellusci. The condition was that they use the same construction material (pollution-resistant Italian travertine), but otherwise each architect was given creative freedom. The buildings' neoclassical exterior elevations give them a certain degree

Metropolitan Opera House

Café des Artistes

*Outside the Museum
of Natural History*

of unity. Lincoln Center was built during the 1960s, and the last building to be completed was the Metropolitan Opera (1966).

Those not eager to see a concert here can still go on a guided tour (*see page 80*). Don't miss the two large murals by Marc Chagall in the foyer of the 'Met'.

From Lincoln Center it's a short walk to the **Museum of American Folk Art** ⓴ (on the corner of Columbus Avenue and 66th Street). This little museum contains various exhibitions devoted to particular themes that are often highly original (admission free).

Walk back up 67th Street in the direction of Central Park; at the junction with Central Park West is the **Hotel des Artistes** ⓴, an establishment which has had several illustrious guests in its time, including Isadora Duncan and Noel Coward. On the ground floor is the famous **Café des Artistes** restaurant, with its European atmosphere and 'old world charm' that Americans love so much.

Enter Central Park now and turn north at the famous **Tavern on the Green**; soon you will arrive at West Drive and **Strawberry Fields** ⓴. This peace garden with plants from 123 countries was created by Yoko Ono in memory of her husband, ex-Beatle John Lennon, who was shot dead in 1980, right outside the **Dakota** where he lived (1 West 72nd Street). Over the years this famous building has remained the grandest residence on Central Park West, attracting tenants like Boris Karloff, Leonard Bernstein and Lauren Bacall (*see pages 68–9*).

A little further along Central Park West is the ★★ **American Museum of Natural History** ⓴. The bombastic facade of this 22-building complex (1872–1933) is reminiscent of a gloomy and forbidding Teutonic fortress. But the 538,000sq ft (50,000sq m) of exhibition space inside is devoted to an impressive series of exhibits on natural history, anthropology and ethnology. The museum is ideal for children: there are enormous dinosaur and whale skeletons; the gem collection contains the largest cut sapphire in the world (the *Star of India*, 463 carats); the Hall of South American Peoples contains shrunken heads and blowpipes; and the **Naturemax Theater** shows films on a screen four stories high and 66ft (20m) wide – the largest cinema screen in the city.

Next door, the **Hayden Planetarium** holds the largest meteorite ever found in the USA, and lovers of contemporary music meet up here on Fridays and Saturdays to enjoy evening laser shows to musical accompaniment.

Should you happen to be visiting the Natural History Museum on a Sunday, it's worth heading for the corner of 77th Street and Columbus afterwards: there's a market selling fresh vegetables, antiques, clothing, toys, comic books, etc.

A walk along 76th Street is a good idea anytime, though: the section between Columbus Avenue and Central Park West is one of the city's numerous historic districts. Those keener on the present than the past are advised to stroll down **Columbus Avenue**. This is a good place to observe the way in which the Upper West Side has changed in recent years. The boutiques, street cafés and tiny bistros are all highly reminiscent of SoHo; yuppies have settled here and left their mark on the area. Old apartments were bought and refurbished, prices went up and what used to be a relatively inexpensive part of the city has become less and less affordable.

Columbus chic

Gentrification is not only evident on Columbus: Amsterdam Avenue and parts of Broadway have also been affected. This section of Broadway has some very fine old apartment houses along it, one such being the **Ansonia** on the corner of 73rd Street. It was built in 1901, and its owners caused quite a stir: they had two swimming pools, real seals frolicking in the fountain in the foyer, and a live bear cruising around the roof-garden.

The Ansonia

Less ostentatious but more architecturally interesting are the **Apthorp Apartments** , which take up the entire block between Broadway, West End Avenue, 78th and 79th Street. They were built for William Waldorf Astor between 1906 and 1908.

71

On the corner of 81st Street and Broadway is a sight of a very different kind: **Zabar's** . To the uninitiated, Zabar's probably looks like just another delicatessen, albeit one with an amazing amount of assorted wares: hundreds of different types of cheese, sausages, imported beers, Italian noodle machines, Chinese woks, French copper saucepans. For New Yorkers, though, Zabar's is a place of pilgrimage and a gourmet paradise. This is where neighborhood residents and non-residents alike meet and exchange the latest news – just like a market-place in medieval times.

Walk further up Broadway from Zabar's and soon some more fine apartment buildings will come into view: the **Belnord** , situated between 86th and 87th Street, Broadway and Amsterdam Avenue, is typical of the Upper West Side, and like the Apthorp, is built around a central courtyard. Between 88th and 90th Street (on the corner with Broadway) stand the impressive **Astor Court Apartments** . From here the route continues via West End Avenue and 88th Street to **Riverside Drive**, the Upper West Side's most majestic boulevard. This street was once lined with magnificent detached villas; the view across leafy Riverside Park had attracted New York's wealthier citizens at the end of the 19th century.

Riverside Park

One mansion still conveys a sense of that era: the **Isaac L Rice Residence** (corner of 89th Street), which was built in 1901. Rice, a well-to-do industrialist, named his home Villa Julia after his wife. Apart from another mansion on 107th Street this is the only detached residence remaining on Riverside Drive; the rest are huge terraced apartment buildings.

In the early years the view of the park and the river was the exclusive domain of WASPs (White Anglo-Saxon Protestants); later on, an increasing number of Jewish families moved into the neighborhood. They were the ones who had 'made it' on the Lower East Side, or who came here to escape Hitler. Washington Heights, further north, also became a refuge for German Jews.

Those interested in art have a good reason to travel north at this point (bus M4). Fort Tryon Park, at West 192nd Street, contains ★ **The Cloisters** (*see map, page 60*), a world away from modern America and totally unexpected in New York: the world of the European Middle Ages. Shifting an entire epoch from one continent to another requires a great deal of money, and the name Rockefeller once again comes as no surprise. During the 1930s, John D Rockefeller Jr had sections of French and Spanish monasteries dismantled, shipped across the Atlantic and reassembled here in the New World. The result is not as barbaric as one would suppose: Romanesque cloisters, Gothic chapels, portals and vaults – the entire architectural history of the Middle Ages stands here in one harmonious ensemble, surrounded by gardens on a hilltop overlooking the Hudson River.

The Cloisters contains the medieval art collection from the Metropolitan Museum of Art (*see pages 65–6*), mostly comprising French, Spanish and Flemish works: stained-glass windows, manuscripts, goldsmiths' work and sculpture, as well as the much-prized Unicorn Tapestries, six handwoven tapestries from the 15th century.

Detail of The Cloisters

The Cloisters

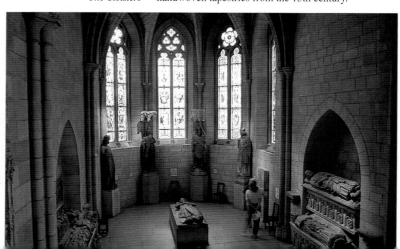

Excursions

Brooklyn – Queens – The Bronx – Staten Island

See map, page 6.

Although Americans always say 'New York' when they actually mean 'Manhattan', the city has four other boroughs. New York City's population of almost 8 million is distributed across all five of them: Manhattan, Brooklyn, the Bronx, Queens and Staten Island. Only 1.5 million or so actually live in Manhattan itself. Its population doubles on weekdays because of commuters from the other boroughs, and also from New Jersey and Connecticut. They arrive on buses, trains and the subway, and their cars stand in traffic jams on the bridges and inside the tunnels. There's a term for them in Manhattan: the B&T ('bridge and tunnel') crowd, and it's not kindly meant. Those who dwell in Manhattan regard it as the spiritual as well as the geographical center of the city. Even residents from other boroughs refer to it as 'The City', and the postal address for Manhattan is 'New York, NY', while the other four boroughs have to be mentioned by their individual names.

There *are* several sights to see in the other boroughs; with all the attractions of Manhattan, though, the problem is actually finding the time. Manhattan's great competitor on the other side of the East River, **Brooklyn**, has several cultural highlights. The **Brooklyn Museum** (*see page 81*), for instance, has a superb Egyptian collection. And few people know that Brooklyn, with its population of 2.3 million, would now be the fourth largest city in the USA if it hadn't been swallowed up by New York in 1898.

You can actually reach Brooklyn on foot, across the famous ★★ **Brooklyn Bridge** (*see page 27*), which was considered the eighth wonder of the world on its completion in 1883. The view of the Manhattan skyline it affords is breathtaking.

Bridge with a view

Those eager to see Manhattan through the eyes of Woody Allen should take a stroll along the **Promenade** in Brooklyn Heights, one of Brooklyn's most attractive neighborhoods. Many artists and intellectuals live in the 19th-century houses here; the rents are almost as high as in Manhattan.

Brooklyn's Promenade

Brooklyn's population is quite a colorful mixture: there is a large Jewish community, more African-Americans live here than in Harlem; there's a large contingent of immigrants from the Caribbean, and some sections, such as 'Little Odessa', are home to Russian and other East European immigrants. Famous Brooklynites include Norman Mailer, Arthur Miller, Barbara Streisand, and Woody Allen.

Coney Island delights

Brooklyn Botanical Gardens

Brooklyn lies on the westernmost tip of Long Island, so it's actually possible to go swimming here, although these days it's not the most savory of prospects: **Coney Island Beach**, the 'poor man's Riviera', is packed on hot summer days, but the water isn't of the highest quality. **Coney Island** itself, formerly one of the largest and most exciting amusement parks in the world, was laid out in the 1880s and thrived until as recently as the 1960s. Coney Island today is a jumble of ugly apartment blocks and empty lots. But all is not lost. There are sideshows by the seashore and a small museum operated by a local theatrical group; Nathan's famous hot dogs are still there to savour, and the sea lions and whales can still be admired at the **New York Aquarium**(Eighth Street/Surf Avenue).

Another popular Brooklyn destination is **Prospect Park**, which, like Central Park, was laid out by Frederick Law Olmsted and Calvert Vaux. To the northeast of the park are the attractive **Brooklyn Botanical Gardens**; across the street is the Brooklyn Museum. Alongside its famous Egyptian collection, the museum also has a vast collection of art from all over the world. In another part of the borough, the **Brooklyn Academy of Music**(30 Lafayette Avenue) enjoys just as good a reputation as the museum, and often hosts theatrical and musical performances with international performers.

To the north of Brooklyn, and also on Long Island, is **Queens**, the largest of New York's boroughs in terms of surface area. Almost 2 million people live here, all of them fast asleep – if Manhattan rumors are to be believed. Queens is considered the 'bedroom' of Manhattan, and is also referred to as 'the borough of cemeteries'. Not that it's necessarily a quiet place: broad highways cut

through endless, monotonous rows of terraced houses, and La Guardia and John F Kennedy airports keep the noise level high.

Every visitor to New York who lands at John F Kennedy International Airport and takes a taxi to Manhattan has to go through Queens. Tennis fans watching television coverage of the US Open from Flushing Meadows Park are actually looking at Queens too, though most don't realize it. Tourists have little reason to go to Queens – unless they are interested in film history. During the silent movie era and the early days of sound, Queens was what Hollywood is today: the center of the motion picture industry. **The American Museum of the Moving Image** (35th Avenue/36th Street, Astoria) brings this era back to life and also has a good deal of information about such modern-day media as TV and video.

A memento from the Museum of the Moving Image

75

Queens may be hard to define, but as far as **The Bronx** is concerned, many associate it with a rough, fairly tough, image. However, not all its population of 1.2 million live behind burned-out facades by any means. Only the southern part of New York's only mainland borough corresponds with the notorious image – and even parts there are experiencing a rebirth; the northern part, with its leafy enclaves along the Hudson River, contains magnificent villas and stately mansions, testifying quite clearly to their owners' wealth. The main attraction of this borough is the **Bronx Zoo/International Wildlife Conservation Park** (Southern Boulevard/Bronx Park South), the largest municipal zoo in the USA. Right next to it are the **New York Botanical Gardens**, originally laid out in 1891 and modeled after Kew Gardens in London.

With a population of just 379,000 and a surface area of 56sq miles (150sq km), **Staten Island** is by far the most thinly-populated of New York's boroughs. It remains somewhat isolated from the other boroughs, and its bucolic atmosphere comes as a refreshing contrast to the bustle and noise of Manhattan. The reason why almost every visitor to Manhattan sets foot on Staten Island at least once is the ferry, which connects the island with Manhattan (*see page 21*). The **Staten Island Ferry** has been in operation since 1840 and until the construction in 1964 of the **Verrazano Narrows Bridge** was the only connection between Staten Island and the other boroughs. The 50-cent round trip is amazingly good value considering the incredible view it provides of the southern tip of Manhattan and its skyline.

Historic Richmond Town

The most interesting sight on Staten Island is the reconstructed village known as **Historic Richmond Town** (441 Clarke Avenue, next to La Tourette Park), an open-air museum documenting life in Richmond – Staten Island's former name – between the 17th and 19th centuries.

Planning and Architecture

City planning in the European sense does not exist in New York. There were no religious or secular despots here eager to realize their visions, and no overall plan. The city's earliest landmarks were responses to the demands of the time, such as the defensive wall to the north, today's Wall Street, or the parade-ground, today's Washington Square. Basically, everyone built what they liked where they liked, or more precisely everyone built what they could afford to build. The city didn't interfere. Grand Central Terminal was built by the Vanderbilts, who owned the railway lines; the city's first opera house was financed by wealthy citizens. Even today's museums, theaters and concert halls are dependent to a large degree on patronage.

The city fathers' first real attempt at city-planning was in 1811, and it had far-reaching consequences: they covered the island of Manhattan with a grid of streets. In so doing, though, they neglected to add any areas of green; the section of the city now occupied by Central Park was only bought back at the behest of several prominent New Yorkers in 1856 – at an astronomical price.

Central Park was bought by prominent New Yorkers

77

The second time the city intervened was in 1916. By this time, 'steel skeleton' construction made it possible to build skyscrapers. The first one in New York was the Flatiron Building, erected in 1902, which was relatively restrained with only 22 storeys. The Equitable Building which appeared on Lower Broadway in 1916 was something else altogether: a monster on an 'H'-shaped ground plan, with 40 floors, and filling an entire block. The walls were perpendicular from top to bottom, without any tiering, and thus the whole neighborhood was plunged into shadow. There were so many complaints that the city found itself compelled to pass a zoning law – the first of its type in the US. It stipulated that the upper floors of a skyscraper should be tiered to allow light through to the streets below. This resulted in the so-called 'wedding-cake' style of building, examples of which include the Chrysler and Empire State Buildings.

The 1902 Flatiron Building

This zoning law was amended in 1961. The cause this time was a building the public liked rather than hated: the Seagram Building, a simple tower with a straight facade on Park Avenue, built by Mies van der Rohe and Philip Johnson in 1958. It followed the rules of the International Style, an extension of the Bauhaus concept. The unusual thing about the scheme was that the architects built a plaza at the foot of the building, over a priceless section of Park Avenue real estate.

It is hard to imagine today how this rather dull plaza could have been such an important innovation, but from then on the law favored skyscrapers that created public

Rockefeller Center:
wonderfully harmonious

1980s excessive Trump Tower

space in this manner. The positive side to this was that peaceful foyers and lobbies were introduced, creating oases of tranquility in midtown or downtown: good examples include the lobby of the IBM Building on Madison Avenue, or the one at the Ford Foundation on 42nd Street. Museums providing free access to the public also qualified as public space under the amendment.

The negative effect of the change in the zoning law can be seen on 6th Avenue, where the western extension of Rockefeller Center consists of four uninviting-looking skyscrapers towering above draughty squares. Rockefeller Center itself, however, is wonderfully harmonious and self-contained: several blocks were designed and built according to a unifying concept, creating one of the world's largest business and entertainment complexes – a 'city within the city' in which tens of thousands of people live and work. The man responsible for this scheme – realized in the middle of the Great Depression – was the multi-millionaire John D Rockefeller Jr.

Another example of successful city-planning can be seen at the southern tip of Manhattan: Battery Park City, built in the 1980s on landfill left over from the construction of the World Trade Center.

The city has been a little too 'trigger-happy' as far as the demolition of fine buildings is concerned. The old Penn Station, for instance, torn down in 1963, formed a fine counterpart to the General Post Office. It was the outcry that followed this which resulted in the Landmark Preservation Act of 1965.

Postmodern architecture in Manhattan is concentrated in the northeastern section of midtown; one of the most interesting buildings here is at 135 East 57th Street. Another example, an elliptical tower known locally as 'the Lipstick Building', is at 885 Third Avenue. Standing next to the IBM Building on Madison is the AT&T Building, now occupied by Sony. It represents a return to more classical ornamentation seen during the 1980s after the austerity of the International Style

After the recession at the end of the 1980s, the 1990s ushered in a new sense of humility and some healthy self-criticism among architects and planners. The city is now learning from past mistakes: the planners responsible for the multi-billion dollar renovation of Times Square, for example, are trying to strike a balance between work and leisure. The related renovation on neighboring 42nd Street seems even more thoughtful and includes a massive overhaul of the subway system.

The fact that city and state are working hand-in-hand on such projects, and not abandoning them to the force of private greed, is something new in New York's history, and shows how open to fresh ideas this city is.

Museums

New York has over 150 museums, most of which are privately run and receive little or no money from public funds. Many ask visitors for contributions towards their upkeep. Here is a list of some of the more famous cultural institutions (note: opening times often change seasonally):

Manhattan
American Museum of Natural History (Central Park West/79th Street). Natural history, ethnology and anthropology. Sunday to Thursday 10am–5.45pm, Friday and Saturday 10am–8.45pm (*see page 70*).

Natural History habitat

   The Cloisters (Fort Tryon Park). Medieval art in reassembled sections of European monasteries. Tuesday to Sunday 9.30am–5.15pm (*see page 72*).

Cloisters column

   Cooper-Hewitt Museum of Design (Fifth Avenue/91st Street). Textiles, jewelry, furniture, graphics, ceramics, etc. Tuesday 10am–9pm, Wednesday to Saturday 10am–5pm, Sunday noon–5pm (*see page 66*).

   Ellis Island Museum (Ellis Island). The history of immigration to the USA. Daily 9.30am–3.30pm, longer in summer. Ferry (Circle Line) leaves hourly from Battery Park, half-hourly in summer (*see page 21*).

   El Museo del Barrio (Fifth Avenue/104th Street). Art and culture of Latin America and Puerto Rico. Wednesday to Sunday 11am–5pm.

   Fraunces Tavern Museum (Pearl/Broad Street). Historic inn, with period furniture from 18th and 19th centuries. Monday to Friday 10am–4.45pm, Saturday noon–4pm (*see page 22*).

   Frick Collection (Fifth Avenue/70th Street). European masterpieces from the 14th–19th centuries. Tuesday to Saturday, 10am–6pm, Sunday 1–6pm (*see page 67*).

Renoir at the Frick
Chagall at the Guggenheim

   Guggenheim Museum (Fifth Avenue/88th Street). Impressionist, Modern and contemporary art in Frank Lloyd Wright's famous building. Daily except Thursday 10am–8pm (*see page 66*). Also in SoHo (575 Broadway). Sunday, Monday, Wednesday 10am–6pm, Thursday to Saturday 11am–8pm (*see page 36*).

   Hayden Planetarium (Central Park West/81st Street). Monday to Friday 12.30–4.45pm, Saturday 10am–5.45pm, Sunday noon–5.45pm (*see page 70*).

   International Center of Photography (Fifth Avenue/94th Street). Photographic exhibitions. Tuesday 11am–8pm, Wednesday to Sunday 11am–6pm.

   Jewish Museum (Fifth Avenue/92nd Street). Historic manuscripts, art and artifacts. Sunday, Monday, Wednesday, Thursday 11am–5.45pm, Tuesday 11am–8pm.

   Lower East Side Tenement Museum (97 Orchard Street). Documents history of Lower East Side immi-

Not to be missed:
the Met

Folk Art at its finest

grants. Tuesday to Friday 11am–5pm, Sunday 10am–5pm (*see page 34*).

Metropolitan Museum of Art (Fifth Avenue/82nd Street). One of the largest and wealthiest museums in the world, full of art from all over the globe. Not to be missed. Tuesday to Thursday, Sunday 9.30am–5.15pm, Friday and Saturday 9.30am–8.45pm (*see pages 65–6*).

Museum of American Folk Art (Columbus Avenue/66th Street). Several fascinating exhibitions. Tuesday to Sunday 11.30am–7.30pm (*see page 70*).

Museum of Modern Art (11 West 53rd Street). Modern art from the 1880s to the present day. Saturday to Tuesday 11am–6pm, Thursday and Friday noon–8.30pm (*see page 51–2*).

Museum of the City of New York (Fifth Avenue/103rd Street). The history of New York from colonization by the Dutch until the present. Wednesday to Saturday 10am–5pm, Sunday 1–5pm.

Pierpont Morgan Library (29 East 36th Street). Paintings, sculpture, manuscripts, all collected by the banker John Pierpont Morgan and his son. Tuesday to Friday 10.30am–5pm, Saturday 10.30am–6pm, Sunday 2–6pm.

Whitney Museum of American Art (Madison Avenue/75th Street). Works by 20th-century American artists. Wednesday, Friday to Sunday 11am–6pm, Thursday 1–8pm (*see page 67*). Also in the Philip Morris Building (Park Avenue/42nd Street). Monday to Friday 11am–6pm, Thursday 11am–7.30pm (*see page 54*).

Other Manhattan museums and attractions

The Dairy (Central Park near West 64th Street). Central Park information and exhibits. Tuesday to Thursday, Saturday, Sunday 11am–5pm, Friday 1–5pm (*see page 64*).

Federal Hall National Memorial (26 Wall Street). Exhibits on George Washington and the new republic. Monday to Friday 9am–5pm (*see page 25*).

Intrepid Sea Air Space Museum (Pier 86 at 12th Avenue and 46th Street. Collection of US Navy missiles and aircraft, on a World War II aircraft carrier. Wednesday to Sunday 10am–5pm.

Lincoln Center for the Performing Arts (Columbus Avenue/64th Street). Guided tours daily starting in concourse (subway station *66th Street/Lincoln Center*), to sign up tel: (212) 875 5350 (*see page 69*).

New York Public Library (Fifth Avenue/42nd Street). Special exhibitions on a number of themes. Tuesday, Wednesday 11am–6pm, Thursday to Saturday 10am–6pm (*see page 55*).

Radio City Music Hall (Sixth Avenue/50th Street). Regular tours of this art-deco palace. Monday to Saturday 10am–4.45pm, Sunday 11am–4.45pm (*see page 51*).

Schomburg Center for Research in Black Culture (515 Lenox Avenue/135th Street). Black literature, history and art. Monday, Tuesday noon–8pm, Wednesday, Friday, Saturday 10am–6pm, Sunday 1–5pm (*see page 59*).

South Street Seaport Museum (Visitors Center, 12 Fulton St). 12-block museum-without-walls, with historic sailing vessels and exhibits, plus shopping and restaurants. Daily 10am–5pm (*see page 26–7*).

United Nations (First Avenue, between 45th and 46th Street). Free tickets to General Assembly plus tours. Daily 9.15am–4.45pm. (*see page 53*).

The Bronx

Bronx Zoo/International Wildlife Conservation Park (Bronx River Parkway/Fordham Road). The country's largest urban zoo. Daily 10am–5pm (*see page 75*).

New York Botanical Gardens (Southern Boulevard at Mosholu Parkway). Acres of attractive landscaped gardens, with classes, lectures and special events. Tuesday to Sunday 10am–6pm (*see page 75*).

Brooklyn

81

Brooklyn Botanical Gardens (100 Washington Avenue, at Prospect Park). A popular garden, with a wonderful conservatory. Tuesday to Friday 8am–4.30pm, Saturady, Sunday and public holidays 10am–4.30pm (*see page 74*).

Brooklyn Children's Museum (145 Brooklyn Avenue). Interactive exhibits for the younger set. Wednesday to Monday 2–5pm.

Brooklyn Museum (200 Eastern Parkway, Prospect Park). Art from all epochs and continents; very good Egyptian collection. Wednesday to Sunday 10am–5pm (*see page 73*).

Queens

American Museum of the Moving Image (35th Avenue/36th Street, Astoria). Historical documentation of the motion picture industry. Tuesday to Friday noon–4pm, Saturday and Sunday noon–6pm (*see page 75*).

Staten Island

Historic Richmond Town (441 Clarke Avenue). Historic village, with costumed guides and buildings dating from the 17th–19th centuries. July and August Wednesday to Friday 10am–5pm, Saturday and Sunday 1–5pm, otherwise Wednesday to Sunday 1–5pm (*see page 75*).

Snug Harbor Cultural Center (1000 Richmond Terrace). An 83-acre combination park, historic site, botanical garden and cultural center, with the Newhouse Center for Contemporary Art here offering a regular schedule of changing exhibits.

Richmond Town restoration

Music and Theater

Don't be afraid of becoming bored in New York. The number and variety of entertainment options available are enormous: open-air concerts in Central Park, jazz in Greenwich Village, cinemas, musicals, Broadway theaters, off-Broadway, off-off-Broadway, the Met, music and dance clubs. To keep pace with what's happening, consult the Friday edition of the *New York Times*, which contains a preview of the forthcoming weekend's events. Weekly publications containing culture sections include the *New York Magazine* (every Monday); *The New Yorker* (every Wednesday), which has a particularly good jazz section; and *The Village Voice* (every Wednesday), which has an excellent guide to events where admission is cheap or free.

Music and dance

New York offers every kind of music and dance imaginable, from opera and classical music to jazz, pop, blues, country, reggae, classical ballet, dance workshops, master classes. Admission to many of the concerts is free: the summer concerts in Central Park, for instance, or the lunch-time concerts held in the Financial District and midtown liven up the day for company employees.

The two largest concert halls in the city are **Carnegie Hall** and **Avery Fisher Hall**; the latter forms part of the **Lincoln Center for the Performing Arts** (*see page 69*), where the **Metropolitan Opera** is also located. Another fine opera company is the **New York City Opera**, which shares the use of the **New York State Theater** (also located in Lincoln Center) with the **New York City Ballet**.

Popular venues for contemporary music include **Madison Square Garden**, **Radio City Music Hall** (*see page 51*), **Symphony Space** on Broadway, the **Town Hall**, the **Beacon Theater** on Broadway and the **Apollo Theater** in Harlem (*see page 59*).

There are numerous dance troupes in the city, like the **Martha Graham Dance Company**, the **Alvin Ailey American Dance Group**, and the **Dance Theater of Harlem**. Dance venues include the **Brooklyn Academy of Music**, the **City Center** on West 55th St, and the **Dance Theater Workshop** on West 19th St.

Concert tickets can be obtained in the same way as theater tickets (*see opposite*). Discount tickets for music and dance events on the same day are available from the **Music & Dance Booth** in Bryant Park, on 42nd Street between Fifth and Sixth avenues (tel: 212-382 2323; Tuesday, Thursday and Friday noon–2pm and 3–7pm; Wednesday and Saturday 11am–2pm and 3–7pm; Sunday noon–6pm). Tickets for Monday concerts are issued the previous day.

The Blue Note is for jazz

Carnegie Hall

Theater

The main Broadway theaters are near Times Square. These stage all the internationally celebrated, large-scale musicals. The alternative to Broadway is off-Broadway, where performances scarcely differ in quality from the former category, albeit performed in smaller theaters. The vast majority of off-Broadway theaters, and indeed, the more experimental off-off-Broadway theaters, are downtown in the Greenwich Village area. Here you'll find the **Public Theater** complex – seven theaters in one building at 425 Lafayette Street, tel: (212) 598 7150 – where *Hair* and *A Chorus Line* originated before being transferred to uptown venues. The **Theater for the New City** at 155 First Ave (tel: 212-254 1109) is one of many showplaces for new work by experimental theater artists.

A few blocks from Times Square, along West 42nd Street between Ninth and Tenth Avenues, a group of off-Broadway theaters have set themselves up as **Theater Row**. The most complete source for off and off-off-Broadway listings is the *Village Voice*. Useful numbers for tickets and/or information are 765-ARTS (2787), a free 24-hour hotline; NYC/On Stage, tel: (212) 768 1818; and The Broadway Line, tel: (212) 563 2929.

Popular shows are often sold out months in advance. Anyone eager to see a particular show should order the tickets via their travel agent before arriving in New York.

There are several ways of getting hold of tickets in New York itself: if you happen to be staying in a good hotel and don't mind tipping generously, the hotel concierge will obtain tickets on your behalf. Otherwise go to the box offices, or to the **Convention & Visitors Bureau** (*see page 98*) where the staff can be of assistance.

Half-price tickets on the day of performance can be obtained from TKTS, which has branches at Times Square and Tower 2 of the World Trade Center. Experience has proved that the lines at the World Trade Center tend to be considerably shorter. The general rule is first come, first served, and reservations aren't possible. Credit cards are not accepted.

TKTS on sale here

Times Square, 47th Street/Broadway: tickets for matinee performances from 10am, for evening performances from 3pm.

Tower 2 World Trade Center, mezzanine level: Monday to Saturday 11am–5.30pm; for off-Broadway 11am–1pm. Limited tickets for matinee and Sunday performances are available on the day prior to as well as the day of performance; tickets for evening performances are only available for events on same day.

The 'Backstage on Broadway' tour provides a behind-the-scenes glimpse of Broadway theater life (*see page 97*).

Food and Drink

Food in New York comes from all over the world. You can eat Brazilian, Italian, French, Indian, Spanish, Korean, Cuban, Turkish, Russian, Jewish, Chinese, Tibetan, Vietnamese and Mexican food, wonderful steaks, great hamburgers, the freshest of seafood, the most organic of health foods. It can be enjoyed in incredibly expensive restaurants or more cheaply in smaller, more humble establishments. The culinary possibilities are unlimited – the city has 17,000 restaurants, cafes, pubs and snack bars!

A good guide through the gastronomic jungle is *Zagat*. An annually updated, sensibly-sized book, it contains restaurant reviews and classifies eateries according to location and specialties served.

Cafe culture

Tips on eating out:

It's always a sensible idea to reserve a table by phone in advance. Wherever this can't be done (eg Chinatown), expect long lines outside many establishments at weekends. Restaurants that happen to be 'in' can often be fully booked whole weeks in advance.

85

Even when a restaurant appears to be empty, don't go straight over to a table and take a seat. 'Wait to be seated' is the local custom. A member of the waiting staff will then come to ask whether you prefer to sit at a smoking or nonsmoking table.

Cakes to go

The service charge isn't usually included in the price, and so a tip isn't to show your appreciation to the waiter – it's his actual wages. This direct payment system has many positive effects: the waiters are almost all friendly, and service is usually very good indeed. Tips in restaurants should be no less than 15 percent of the total price of the meal (it's easy to work out this figure in New York: just double the amount shown as 'tax'). If you feel the service was unsatisfactory, reduce the percentage. It is customary to leave the gratuity lying on the table in cash after you have paid the bill.

Beware, though: some waiters who know they're serving tourists will add their tip to the final amount in advance, so check first to see whether service has already been included.

Service with a smile

If the waiter brings the bill without being asked, it is a sign to vacate your table. This is not like other cities, where you can carry on sitting and talking over a drink. Restaurant owners keep a steady eye on their turnover, and their next customers are likely to be waiting for the table – business, after all, is business.

The helpings are almost always enormous. If you can't finish all the food on your plage, don't be embarassed to ask for a 'doggy bag.'

Lower East Side diner

Meal times

New York breakfasts can be huge, with fried eggs, bacon, sausages, pancakes covered with maple syrup, cornflakes and, of course, toast and jam or marmalade. Lunches are somewhat less filling, usually for professional reasons. Businessmen in New York tend to grab a sandwich from the local 'deli' or eat a quick meal at a coffee shop or fast-food outlet.

The main meal of the day is dinner, usually preceded by a drink at the bar. Sunday brunch – a late breakfast which can often last until early afternoon – is a New York institution. A lot of establishments, including the large hotel restaurants, offer their own brunch specialties on Sundays. One good place to go for brunch is Chinatown, where tiny steamed delicacies known as *dim-sum* can be consumed in vast quantities.

Drinks

Not all restaurants have liquor licenses. Several of the smaller, cheaper establishments advertise themselves as 'BYOB' – 'bring your own bottle' – meaning that you can

buy your own wine or beer in the local supermarket and are then given a corkscrew and a glass by the restaurateur. Meals in these establishments work out a lot cheaper than in fully-licensed restaurants, where alcohol is often very expensive. Lots of places serve Californian wines, whose quality remains remarkably consistent. Beer is either served in bottles or 'on tap' (ie draught).

Coffee used to be on the weak side for European tastes, but this is no longer necessarily the case. It usually gets served at no extra charge; just ask for a refill.

Men at work

Broome Street Bar detail

Restaurants

Below is a small selection of some of New York's better restaurants:

Le Bernadin, 155 West 51st Street, tel: (212) 489 1515; though expensive, this is the best French seafood restaurant in the city.

Bouley, 165 Duane Street, TriBeCa, tel: (212) 608 3852; this is one of the top restaurants in town, beloved of gourmets: the cook, David Bouley, is a Bocuse pupil. Very expensive.

Broome Street Bar, 363 West Broadway, SoHo, tel: (212) 925 2086; one of the oldest bars in the neighborhood, which was in business before SoHo became so chic. Especially good hamburgers.

B. Smith's, 771 Eighth Avenue, tel: (212) 247 2222; an excellent Theater District choice – chic but not too expensive, and specializes in Southern-style cooking.

Cucina Stagionale, 275 Bleecker Street, Greenwich Village, tel: (212) 924 2707; a very popular BYOB restaurant in the Village, serving excellent-value and delicious Italian food.

Ferrara, 195 Grand Street, Little Italy, tel: (212) 226 6150; a good place to wander to after a meal in Chinatown. The cakes here are famous.

Hard Rock Café, 221 West 57th Street, tel: (212) 459 9320; a mainly young clientele enjoys the high-decibel ambience here; great hamburgers, however.

Hatsuhana, 17 East 48th Street, (between Fifth Avenue and Madison Avenue), tel: (212) 335 3345; the best Japanese *sushi* and *sashimi* restaurant in the city. A must for raw fish enthusiasts.

Kiev, 117 Second Avenue, East Village, tel: (212) 674 4040; an unpretentious establishment serving excellent Jewish and East European fare.

Nice, 35 East Broadway (near Catherine Street), tel: (212) 406 9776; this Chinese restaurant is the place to go to sample some *dim-sum.* It's cheaper than its main competitor across the street, **The Golden Unicorn** (also highly recommended).

The Oyster Bar, Grand Central Terminal, Vanderbilt Avenue/42nd Street, tel: (212) 490 6650; superb seafood – the best in town.

Rikyu, 210 Columbus Avenue, Upper West Side, tel: (212) 799 7847; another excellent Japanese restaurant (cf **Hatsuhana** above).

Rosa Mexicano, 1063 First Avenue (58th Street),tel: (212) 753 7407; serves the best Mexican food in New York. Great Margaritas too. Make sure you reserve well in advance.

Spark's Steakhouse, 210 East 46th Street, tel: (212) 687 4855; not only excellent steaks, but very fine wines too. Expensive.

Tavern on the Green, Central Park West/67th Street, tel: (212) 873 3200; wonderfully situated on Central Park. International cuisine. The trees are hung with thousands of lights. Romantic, fashionable – and expensive.

Tavern on the Green

The Russian Tea Rooms, 150 West 57th Street (near Seventh Avenue), tel: (212) 265 0947; popular with celebrities (Woody Allen, Isaac Stern, Liza Minelli, etc). Good Russian food. Expensive.

The SoHo Kitchen and Bar, 103 Greene Street, SoHo, tel: (212) 925 1866; a very typical SoHo restaurant with high tiled walls and a long counter.

SoHo Kitchen and Bar

Union Square Café, 21 East 16th Street, tel: (212) 243 4020; offers Italian, French and American food. Dishes are delicious and sensibly priced too. Not to be missed.

Zen Palate, 663 Ninth Avenue/46th Street, tel: (212) 582 1669; this is one of the best vegetarian restaurants in the whole of Manhattan. Delicious, creative cuisine. No alcohol.

Wooden wares for sale

Shopping

Manhattan's busiest shopping streets are its avenues; they are a consumer's paradise. The only mid-to-uptown areas still relatively peaceful and free of crowds are Central Park West, the section of Fifth Avenue next to Central Park, and Park Avenue. The smaller stores – newsagents, supermarkets, grocery stores, dry cleaners, etc – tend to be found all over neighborhoods like the Upper West Side, Upper East Side, Harlem, Greenwich Village, Chelsea, etc. Most Manhattan residents have no car; they either buy necessities from the nearest store in their neighborhood, or they have the store deliver provisions to their apartments.

The most exclusive shops are on Madison Avenue, between 60th and 79th Streets; on 57th Street between Lexington and Sixth Avenues; and in the 50s blocks of Fifth Avenue. Fifth Avenue also contains cheap stores peddling discount electronic goods, leather goods, Asian vases and other imported articles.

Boutiques with avant-garde fashions, original gifts and souvenirs, children's fashions, toys and other essentials can be found along Columbus Avenue, and also Amsterdam Avenue between 66th and 84th Streets. The city's jewelers are concentrated on 47th Street, in the section of it known as 'Diamond Row.'

Shop till you drop

The Village and SoHo have several eccentric stores with unusual window displays. Many of the city's galleries are here too. Almost everything in Chinatown, on the other hand, is 'made in Taiwan.'

On Sunday there's a very busy street market on Orchard Street, on the Lower East Side (*see page 34*): this is the place to come for discount clothing, shoes and leather goods. Be prepared to haggle, too. Stay away from here on Saturday, when the whole place is deserted.

Another flea market (one of several around the city) is held every Sunday on the Upper West Side, on the corner of Columbus Avenue and 77th Street.

Anyone keen on specialist shops is advised to buy a copy of Gerry Frank's *Where to Find It, Buy It, Eat It*.

Books

Most of the major publishers in the USA have their headquarters in New York. The city also has a plethora of bookstores, including:

Barnes & Noble, several branches throughout the city. Discount books, bestsellers.

Eeyore's, 2212 Broadway/79th Street. Good assortment of children's books.

Gotham Book Mart, 41 West 47th Street. A great place to browse.

Strand Bookstore, 828 Broadway/12th Street. One of the last survivors of what was once known as 'Booksellers' Row'. Superb selection of used books.

Department Stores

Barney's, Madison Avenue/61st Street.

Bloomingdale's, Lexington Avenue/59th Street.

Lord & Taylor, Fifth Avenue and 39th Street.

Macy's, Herald Square.

Saks, Fifth Avenue, 611 Fifth Avenue.

Electronics

Photographic goods and video recorders, CD players, etc are all very good value in New York. Try:

47th Street Photo, 67 West 47th Street. Cameras, computers, etc. Closed Saturday.

Jeans

Canal Jeans, 504 Broadway, between Broome and Spring Streets. Jeans, T-shirts, sweatshirts.

Museum Shops

The MOMA Design Store, 44 West 53rd Street. Designer furniture, household articles.

Metropolitan Museum of Art Gift Shop, in the museum on Fifth Avenue and also at Rockefeller Center (610 Fifth Avenue). Art books, posters, jewelry, reproductions.

Records, tapes, CDs

Tower Records, 692 Broadway/East 4th Street. The place to go. Huge selection. Great discounts.

Toys

FAO Schwarz, 767 Fifth Avenue. The Fifth Avenue branch of America's most famous toyshop.

Strand Bookstore

89

Macy's

MOMA store

Decked out for the evening

Nightlife

Nightlife in New York tends to get under way at around 11pm, not before. Most of the city's nightclubs are extremely short-lived. Discos, bars and clubs that are 'in' one month are usually 'out' the next. The only way to find out is to do your own research on the spot, and then hope to be admitted by the stony-faced, all-powerful doorman. This is no easy task: the 'right' clothes may help.

Dance Clubs

CBGB & OMFUG
315 Bowery at Bleecker Street
The club where punk started in America.

Club USA
218 West 47th Street
An enormous multi-level funhouse near Times Square.

Limelight
660 Sixth Avenue
Dancing inside a neo-Gothic church.

Palladium
126 East 14th Street
Not quite as 'in' as it used to be, but still impressive.

The Pyramid Club

The Pyramid Club
101 Avenue A
Typical East Village establishment, only for the hard-core.

Club scene

S.O.B.'s
204 Varick Street
A SoHo bastion of Latin-American sounds.

Sweetwaters
170 Amsterdam at 68th Street
Dining and dancing for the well-heeled.

Webster Hall
125 East 11th Street
A large club in East Village, less slick than most. All-night dancing to everything from rock and reggae to house.

Wetlands
161 Hudson Street below Canal
Casual club in TriBeCa for grooving to the sounds of the 60s, as well as reggae, folk, jazz and funk.

Jazz Clubs

New York holds a special fascination for jazz lovers. The following classic jazz clubs are all in the West Village:

Hot sounds for a cool clientele

Blue Note, 131 West 3rd Street
The very best of mainstream jazz and blues, from time-honored greats to more contemporary acts.

Sweet Basil
88 Seventh Avenue South
Another venue for fine mainstream jazz.

Village Vanguard
178 Seventh Avenue South
The club that helped to launch legendary talents like Miles Davis and John Coltrane.

Bars

Chumley's
86 Bedford Street
A 'speakeasy' from Prohibition days.

McSorley's Old Ale House
15 East Seventh Avenue
Old-fashioned tavern with sawdust floors.

Oak Room in the Plaza Hotel
Fifth Avenue/59th Street
Cozy club atmosphere.

PJ Clarke's
915 Third Avenue
Aging singles eager not to remain single for much longer.

Getting There

By Plane

There are a number of ways to get to Manhattan (15 miles/24km away) from **John F Kennedy International Airport** in Queens.

The cheapest is to take the shuttle bus (5am–midnight every 10 minutes, otherwise every 30 minutes) to the Howard Beach/JFK Airport subway station, which connects directly with Manhattan. However, if you're unfamiliar with the subway system, take the slightly more expensive **Carey Airport Express Coach Buses** to midtown Manhattan (every 30 minutes 6am–midnight). The fare is under $15; for more information, tel: 718-632 0509.

Carey Airport Express

Gray Line Air Shuttle minibuses (daily, 7am–11pm) stop at most hotels in Manhattan between 23rd and 63rd Streets and are slightly more expensive. For more information, tel: (212) 315 3006.

The most comfortable way to Manhattan is by taxi. This costs $30–40, plus bridge and tunnel tolls and a 15 percent tip. Ride only in yellow (licensed) cabs.

The city's other international airport, **Newark International**, lies 16 miles (26km) east of Manhattan, in New Jersey. There are bus connections from here (including **Olympic Trails Export Express Bus**, tel: (212) 964 6233 or 908-354 3330 to Pennsylvania Station, to Grand Central Terminal (every 20 minutes, 6.15am–midnight) and to the World Trade Center (every 30 minutes, 6.45am–10.45pm). The **Gray Line Air Shuttle** minibuses (7am–11pm) stop at several hotels in Manhattan. The taxi fare from Newark is approximately $40; in the other direction, it is the amount on the meter plus $10. Bridge and tunnel tolls are extra, as is a 15 percent tip.

Domestic flights land at **La Guardia Airport**, only 8 miles (13km) east of midtown Manhattan in Queens. **Carey Airport Express Coach Bus** (every 30 minutes, 6.45am–midnight) connects with midtown Manhattan; **Gray Line Air Shuttle** minibuses connect with several hotels in Manhattan; and taxis usually cost less than $30, with bridge and tunnel tolls (and 15 percent tip) extra.

By Train

Long distance Amtrak trains arrive at and depart from **Pennsylvania Station** (Seventh Avenue/32nd Street), as do commuter trains to and from Long Island. **Grand Central** (Park Avenue/42nd Street) is generally for commuter trains only.

By Bus

All buses arrive at the **Port Authority Bus Terminal** (Eighth Avenue/41st Street).

Getting Around

Orientation

Getting your bearings in Manhattan is remarkably easy. Apart from Lower Manhattan, where the thoroughfares twist and turn, and can even have individual names, all the straight thoroughfares running from west to east are called 'streets' and are numbered from south to north (1st, 2nd, 3rd, etc). In addresses, the addition of a 'West' (W) or an 'East' (E) after the address number show whether it lies to the west or east of Fifth Avenue.

The avenues run north-south, intersecting with the streets at right angles. They too are numbered, from (starting in the east) First to Twelfth Avenue. Some have their own names, eg York Avenue, Lexington Avenue, Park Avenue and Madison Avenue; and Sixth Avenue is officially called Avenue of the Americas. There's just one street that doesn't conform to this pattern: Broadway cuts across the island diagonally.

Don't rent a car. Parking spaces are almost non-existent and you will soon become a victim of gridlock.

Underground opportunities

The New York subway

The New York subway has a bad reputation. The crimes which regularly hit the headlines only seem to confirm this. But when one considers that 3.3 million people use the subway each day without problem, there seems to be no reason not to use it. It is the fastest way of getting around, and the city couldn't function without it.

As far as your personal safety on the subway is concerned, a few basic rules should be followed:

- Don't take the subway to parts of the city tourists don't normally go (Harlem, the Bronx, etc).
- Always stick with the crowd whenever you get on or off a train. Avoid remote entrances or exits.
- Have the exact amount of money for the trip ready; keep your wallet or purse hidden.
- Don't get into carriages that are empty or unilluminated.
- Remember to keep a firm grip on your bags.

A subway token costs $1.25 and is bought at the official booth in the station. A single fare allows you to travel as far as you like. Check the direction you're traveling in: *downtown* (southwards), *uptown* (northwards) or *crosstown*. Express trains leave out certain stations, local trains stop everywhere.

Traveling at peak times (7.30–9am and 4.30–7pm) is not recommended, unless you happen to be fond of crowds. Free subway maps are sometimes available from the token booths.

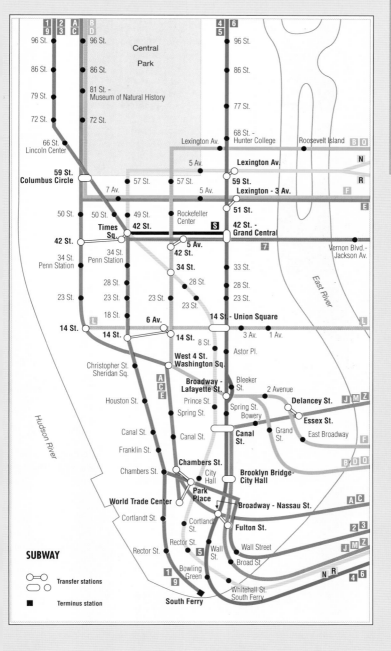

SUBWAY

⊙—⊙ Transfer stations
⊙ ⊙

■ Terminus station

Buses

Buses are safer and generally more pleasant than the subway, and they connect most of Manhattan's east-west streets (the subway is north-south oriented).

A bus trip costs either $1.25 or one token. Have the exact amount ready – drivers provide no change. If you want to change on the journey ask the driver for a free transfer ticket, which you can use for the next bus.

Manhattan bus maps are (sometimes) available from token booths at subways, or from the New York Convention & Visitors Bureau on Columbus Circle. For information about subways and buses, tel: (212) 330 1234.

Getting from Times Square to TriBeCa

Taxis

These have to be hailed. There are no taxi ranks in New York, and only private car services can be ordered by phone. Before setting off in a cab make sure the driver knows your destination.

All licensed (ie yellow) taxis have electronic meters that print out receipts if required. A tip of 15 percent is expected. Beware of unlicensed cabs which are not yellow and have no meter: their fares are extortionate.

For information about taxis, tel: (212) 830 TAXI.

Motorists

Driving to New York isn't recommended, mainly because parking is expensive (in garages or lots) and either risky or unavailable (on the streets).

Roads outside New York are in good condition. The road system in the US consists of Interstate Freeways (eg I-84), United States Highways (eg US95), State Highways or Routes (country roads) and Secondary State or County Roads (side roads).

The maximum speed limit outside urban areas is 55mph (88kmph), 65mph (105kmph) in some states and 25–30mph (40–48kmph) in built-up areas unless otherwise indicated. School buses that are stationary with their lights flashing may *not* be overtaken.

Car rental

To rent a car in New York you have to be over 21 years of age and have a national driving license, though an international one is best. Some car rental firms add a surcharge for drivers aged under 25.

If you are considering renting a car, check out the conditions. It's good to use larger firms in case the vehicle has to be exchanged at any point. **Credit cards** are necessary for all car rentals in the US.

Toll-free (1)-800 numbers for central reservations can be found in the *Yellow Pages* under **Car** or **Automobile Rentals** (Avis, Budget, Hertz, etc).

Sightseeing tours (a selection)

Bus

- Gray Line, 1740 Broadway, tel: (212) 397 2620. One of the most well-known bus companies with a wide range of tours. Tours last between two and eight hours.
- Gray Line New York Trolley, 254 West 57th Street, tel: (212) 397 3807.
- Manhattan Double Decker Tours, 10 East 39th Street, tel: (212) 679 8104.
- New York Apple Tours Inc., tel: (1- 800) 876 9868. Get on and off the double decker buses as often as you like; tours include the 'Statue of Liberty Express'.

Touring around town

Boat

- Circle Line Sightseeing, Pier 83 at the western end of 42nd Street, tel: (212) 563 3200. A three-hour trip around the entire island, showing all aspects of Manhattan from the water. Daily March–December.
- Staten Island Ferry. *(see page 21)* Runs between Battery Park and Staten Island; the cheapest way to see the Manhattan skyline from the water: 50¢ return!

Helicopter

- Island Helicopter Sightseeing, heliport at eastern end of 34th Street, tel: (212) 683 4575. Manhattan from the sky – not exactly cheap, but exhilarating.

On Foot

- Walk of the Town, 280 Riverside Drive, tel: (212) 222 5343. Tours through particular neighborhoods and also guided tours on special themes, eg sights and buildings with literary associations.
- Citywalks, 410 West 20th Street, tel: (212) 989 2456. Two-hour-long guided tours of downtown, Greenwich Village, midtown or Lower East Side as seen through the eyes of local residents.

Guided tours with special themes

- Harlem, Your Way! Tours Unlimited, 129 West 130th Street, tel: (212) 690 1687. Offers guided tours of Harlem, including evening tours featuring a visit to renowned Apollo Theater, a Sunday gospel program, and visits to galleries.
- Harlem Spirituals, 1697 Broadway, tel: (212) 757 0425. Jazz and gospel tours.
- Backstage on Broadway, 228 West 47th Street, tel: (212) 575 8065. A look behind the scenes at Broadway's greatest theaters.
- Inside New York, 203 East 72nd Street, tel: (212) 861 0709. An introduction to the New York fashion world; tour includes a fashion show and chance to buy goods.

97

Facts for the Visitor

Travel Documents

International travelers should bring a valid **passport**. No visa is required if your length of stay does not exceed 90 days and you can furnish a valid return ticket. If you want to stay longer, apply for a visa at the US Consulate.

Length of stay is determined by the immigration officer you meet on arrival, so it's a good idea to have ready such things as credit cards, traveler's checks or hotel reservation forms if requested to do so.

Customs

Items for personal use can be brought into the USA duty-free. Duty-free allowances include 200 cigarettes or 50 cigars or 2kg of tobacco; 11 alcoholic drinks and presents to a value of $100.

Flowers, meat, vegetables or fruit may not be brought into the country.

Tourist information

In New York, information and brochures about hotels, restaurants, sightseeing etc are available from **The New York Convention & Visitors Bureau**, 2 Columbus Circle, tel: (212) 397 8222 (Monday–Friday 9am–6pm, Saturday and Sunday 10am–6pm).

Detailed maps of the city (showing subway lines and bus routes) and also travel guides can be purchased at the **Hagstrom Map & Travel Center**, 57 West 43rd Street, tel: (212) 398 1222.

Foreign affairs

Currency & exchange

The unit of currency in the US is the dollar ($) = 100 cents (¢). The following coins are in circulation at present: cent (1¢); nickel (5¢); dime (10¢); quarter (25¢); half-dollar (50¢); and $1. Banknotes come in the following denominations: $1, $2, $5, $10, $20, $50, $100 and up. They are all the same size and color, and the only way to tell them apart is by the printed value and different presidents depicted.

There is no limit to the amount of foreign or domestic currency that can be taken in or out of the country; travelers checks or cash worth more than $100,000 must be declared, however.

It's best to bring a credit card (eg Visa, MasterCard), US dollar travelers checks for small sums ($20, $50), and also a small amount of cash in low-denomination notes. Most hotels, restaurants and shops accept US dollar travelers checks and most banks will convert them into cash. American visitors can use out of state bankcards in the automatic teller machines.

Opening times

Store owners in New York decide when they want to close – there's no mandatory closing time. Large department stores in midtown close on Sunday, and the Jewish-run shops on Orchard Street close on Saturday.

Banks: Usually Monday to Friday 9am–3pm, and on one day in the week (usually Thursday) until 6pm; a few are also open on Saturday mornings.

Post Offices: Monday to Friday 9am–6pm, Saturday 8am–noon; General Post Office daily 7.30am–8pm.

Public holidays

New Year's Day (January 1); Martin Luther King Day (3rd Monday in January); Washington's Birthday (3rd Monday in February); Memorial Day (last Monday in May); Independence Day (July 4); Labor Day (1st Monday in September); Columbus Day (2nd Monday in October); Veterans' Day (November 11); Thanksgiving Day (4th Thursday in November); Christmas Day (December 25).

There are local public holidays too. If a holiday falls on a Sunday, the Monday after is also a holiday and post offices, government offices, etc are closed.

Tax

Value added tax is never included in the prices displayed at tills in New York, therefore, you pay the basic price plus 8.25 percent sales tax. The tax authorities are particularly greedy where hotel bills are concerned: 14.25 percent is charged on rooms under $100 a night, and 19.25 percent on rooms costing over $100. This so-called room tax is supplemented still further by a transient occupancy tax of $2 a night.

Telephone

Phone home from here

Local calls (25¢) can easily be made from phone booths (just follow the printed instructions). **Long-distance calls** have to be made via the operator (dial 0) unless you know the area code and the number, in which case you can dial directly. **Overseas calls** can also be made directly, but if you're calling from a pay phone your pockets will have to be stuffed full of quarters. If in doubt ring the overseas operator (dial 0). The code for the UK is 0 11 44 followed by the area code minus the first zero, and then the actual number. **Telegrams** can be placed with Western Union or via hotel reception.

There are two area codes for New York: 212 for Manhattan, and 718 for Brooklyn, Queens, Staten Island and the Bronx.

Important telephone numbers:
Emergency (fire, police, ambulance): tel: 911
Deaf Emergency Line: tel: (1-800) 342 4357.

Temperature

Temperature reports are in Fahrenheit. To convert to Centigrade:subtract 32, then divide by 9 and multiply by 5.
(0°C = 32°F, 10°C = 50°F, 20°C = 68°F, 30°C = 86°F, etc.)

Voltage

110v AC. Adaptors can be bought at most airports as well as local hardware stores.

Time

New York is on Eastern Standard Time (5 hours behind London). Daylight saving time is from the beginning of April until the end of October.

Tipping

Waiters in restaurants expect at least 15 percent of the bill to be placed on the table after a meal. In hotels, bellmen should be given around $1 a bag, and a bit extra if they have to go a long way; doormen expect $1 for merely opening car doors or calling cabs; chambermaids get $1 a night for routine cleaning; taxi drivers get 15 percent of the bill; shoe-cleaners and cloakroom attendants get $1 each; and at the bar, 50¢ per drink.

Medical assistance

Medical help has to be paid for instantly, either in cash or by credit card. Europeans and other non-US citizens are strongly advised to take out medical insurance.

24-hour Pharmacy: Kaufmann Pharmacy, Lexington Avenue/50th Street, tel: (212) 755 2266.

The NYPD

Security Precautions

New York is certainly not the safest of cities, but it's a lot safer than is often suggested. If you follow a few basic rules you won't encounter many problems.

- Avoid wearing expensive jewelry or expensive-looking jackets.
- Don't accept offers from strangers to carry your luggage.
- Use the hotel safe wherever possible.
- In hotel rooms, use the peephole in the door to check out callers before opening.
- Never carry large amounts of cash. Almost all establishments accept credit cards and travelers checks.
- If the character of a street starts to change, turn back immediately.
- If you get mugged, offer no resistance.

Alcohol

The minimum age for consumption of alcoholic beverages is 21.

Where to Stay

One of the city's grand hotels

Staying in New York is not cheap. Anything more comfortable than a youth hostel usually costs at least $100 a night and up. Luxury hotels cost three times that figure.

The state and city levies are high, and sales and room taxes add from 14 to 20 percent to room bills, with an extra 'transient occupancy tax' of $2 per night tagged on for no good reason.

Tipping is expected: bellmen should be given around $1 a bag, and a bit extra if they have to go a long way; doormen expect $1 for merely opening car doors or calling cabs; waiters get 15 percent of the bill; chambermaids get $1 a night for routine cleaning.

Making a phone call from your hotel can be astronomically expensive, with most establishments charging incredibly high rates. Check first. Phone booths are far cheaper, even though filling them with coins can often be tiresome (see page 99).

The following list is a selection from the various categories, from very expensive ($$$$$) to cheap ($$):

$$$$$
(Double rooms from $300)

New York's two world-famous hotels are **The Plaza** and the **Waldorf-Astoria**. Each lobby has been meticulously restored to a standard similar to that in their heyday; bedrooms can be small, however.

The Plaza

The Plaza, Fifth Avenue/59th Street, NY 10019; tel: (212) 759 3000, fax: (212) 759 3160; **Waldorf-Astoria**, Park Avenue/50th Street, NY 10022; tel: (212) 355 3000, fax: (212) 758 2809.

Those expecting discreet luxury, impeccable service and a distinguished yet friendly ambiance should consider either of the following:

Plaza Athenée, 37 East 64th Street, NY 10021, tel:

(212) 734-9100, fax: (212) 772 0958; **Pierre**, Fifth Avenue/61st Street, NY 10021, tel: (212) 838 8000, fax: (212) 940 8109.

$$$$

(Double rooms from $100–$300)

The Algonquin

Algonquin, 59 West 44th Street, NY 10036, tel: (212) 840 6800, fax: (212) 944 1419; **Beverly**, 125 East 50th Street, NY 10022, tel: (212) 753 2700; **Doral Inn**, 541 Lexington Avenue, NY 10022, tel: (212) 755 1200, fax: (212) 319 8344; **Lexington Hotel,** Lexington Avenue/48th Street, NY 10017, tel: (212) 755 4400, fax: (212) 751 4091; **Mayflower**, 15 Central Park West/61st Street, NY 10023, tel: (212) 265 0060, fax: (212) 265 5098; **Paramount**, 235 West 46th Street, NY 10036, tel: (212) 764 5500, fax: (212) 354 5237; **Radisson Empire,** 44 West 63rd Street, NY 10023, tel: (212) 265 7400, fax: (212) 765 4913; **Roger Smith,** 501 Lexington Avenue/47th Street, NY 10017, tel: (212) 755 1400, fax: (212) 319 9130; **St Moritz,** 50 Central Park South, NY 10019, tel: (212) 755 5800, fax: (212) 751 2952.

$$$

(Double rooms from $100–$160)

Comfort Inn Murray Hill, 42 West 35th Street, NY 10001, tel: (212) 947 0200, fax: (212) 594 3047; **Franklin**, 164 East 87th Street, NY 10128, tel: (212) 369 1000, fax: (212) 369 8000; **Milford Plaza (Ramada Hotel)**, 270 West 45th Street, NY 10036, tel: (212) 869 3600, fax: (212) 944 8357; **Salisbury**, 123 West 57th Street, NY 10019, tel: (212) 246 1300, fax: (212) 977 7752; **Wyndham**, 42 West 58th Street, NY 10019, tel: (212) 753 3500; **Helmsley Windsor**, 100 West 58th Street, NY 10019, tel: (212) 265 2100, fax: (212) 315 0371.

$$

(Double rooms starting under $100)

Washington Square Hotel

Broadway American, 2178 Broadway, NY 10024, tel: (212) 362 1100, fax: (212) 787 9521; **Chelsea Inn**, 46 West 17th Street, NY 10011, tel: (212) 645 8989, fax: (212) 987 3307; **Pickwick Arms**, 230 East 51st Street, NY 10022, tel: (212) 355 0300, fax: (212) 755 5029; **Washington Square Hotel**, 103 Waverly Place, NY 10011, tel: (212) 777 9515, fax: (212) 979 8373.

Suite Hotels

For $200–$400 a night it's possible to rent a small suite, providing an extra bed alongside the double – ideal for families. These suites are like mini-apartments, with a kitchen niche equipped for self-catering – a useful way of saving money.

Beekman Tower, 3 Mitchell Place, First Avenue/49th Street, NY 10017, tel: (212) 355 7300, fax: (212) 753 9366; **Dumont Plaza**, 150 East 34th Street, NY 10016, tel: (212) 481 7600, fax: (212) 889 8856; **Eastgate Tower**, 222 East 39th Street, NY 10016, tel: (212) 687 8000, fax: (212) 490 2634; **Lyden Gardens**, 215 East 64th Street, NY 10021, tel: (212) 355 1230, fax: (212) 758 7858; **Plaza Fifty**, 155 East 50th Street, NY 10022, tel: (212) 751 5710, fax: (212) 753 1468; **Shelburne,** 303 Lexington Avenue/37th Street, NY 10016, tel: (212) 689 5200, fax: (212) 779 7068; **Southgate Tower**, 371 Seventh Avenue/31st Street, NY 10001, tel: (212) 563 1800, fax: (212) 643 8028; **Surrey**, 20 East 76th Street, NY 10021, tel: (212) 288 3700, fax: (212) 628 1594.

Suites at all these hotels can be reserved through the central reservation number for **Manhattan East Suite Hotels**: tel: (212) 465 3690, toll-free: (1- 800) 637 8483.

YMCA/YWCA

(Double rooms from $50)
Accommodation at the **Young Men's Christian Association** is available to both men and women. Reservations should be made well in advance.

YMCA-West Side, 5 West 63rd Street, NY 10023, tel: (212) 787 4400; **Vanderbilt YMCA**, 227 East 47th Street, NY 10017, tel: (212) 756 9600.

Youth Hostels

(Around $20)
Stays at the city's main youth hostel are limited to seven days. Reservations should be made well in advance. There's no age restriction. Discounts are available for members of youth hostel associations (with international identity cards). Dormitories sleep 4–12 people.

New York International Youth Hostel, 891 Amsterdam Avenue/103rd Street, NY 10025, tel: (212) 932 2300, fax: (212) 932 2574.

Bed and Breakfast

B&B is a relatively recent phenomenon in the city and a very good way of getting to know the locals. Whole apartments can be rented, or rooms in private homes. It often involves sharing the bathroom with the landlord, but that's only a small sacrifice in return for the personal contact and wealth of information available.

B&B accommodation is often cheaper than medium-priced hotel accommodation, especially since the taxes and surcharges don't apply.

For more information, try calling the **B&B Network of New York**, tel: (212) 645 8134 or **City Lights Bed & Breakfast Ltd.**, tel: (212) 737 7049.

Tips gratefully received

Index